How to Lead Work Teams

How to Lead Work Teams

Facilitation Skills
Second Edition

Fran Rees

Pfeiffer
A Wiley Imprint
www.pfeiffer.com

Published by Pfeiffer
A Wiley Imprint
989 Market Street, San Francisco, CA 94103-1741   www.pfeiffer.com

Pfeiffer books and products are available through most bookstores. To contact Pfeiffer directly call our Customer Care Department within the U.S. at 800-956-7739, outside the U.S. at 317-572-3986, or fax 317-572-4002.

Pfeiffer also publishes its books in a variety of electronic formats. Some content that appears in print may not be available in electronic books.

Library of Congress Cataloging-in-Publication Data

Rees, Fran.
  How to lead work teams : facilitation skills / Fran Rees.— 2nd
ed.
    p. cm.
  Includes bibliographical references and index.
  ISBN 0-7879-5691-0 (alk. paper)
  1. Teams in the workplace—Management. 2. Group facilitation.
I. Title.
  HD66 .R394 2001
  658.4'036—dc21   00-013136

Printed in the United States of America

Acquiring Editor: Josh Blatter
Director of Development: Kathleen Dolan Davies
Developmental Editor: Susan Rachmeler
Editor: Rebecca Taff
Senior Production Editor: Dawn Kilgore
Manufacturing Supervisor: Becky Carreño
Cover Design: Bruce Lundquist

Printing   10 9 8 7 6 5 4 3 2

Contents

Introduction

As we enter a new century, the dynamics of change have shifted the emphasis from "teams" as discrete units with boundaries and responsibilities to an emphasis on "teamwork" across all organizational boundaries. The "high performing" teams of the 1990s are more commonplace in the corporate structures of today. Indeed, some organizations resemble the high performing teams of several years ago.

How to Lead Work Teams: Facilitation Skills (1991) was written to help managers and team leaders make the transition from traditional "manager" to "team leader." The first edition focused on intact work teams and encouraged team leaders to use group process and facilitation methods to solve problems and improve quality.

This, the second edition, focuses on leading *teamwork* in dynamic, responsive, and change-driven organizations. Today, leaders must lead in faster-paced arenas, in more volatile markets, with fewer precedents, and with even greater consequences. Facilitative leaders are even more necessary than they were ten years ago. Teams are pervasive and dynamic, and teamwork is required in broader arenas. The purpose of this book is to help leaders develop fundamental facilitation skills and attitudes, which will guide them in developing high performing organizations through teamwork.

The audience for this edition is anyone who must take a leadership role to get his or her work done. Team leaders, project leaders, managers, individual contributors, human resources professionals, organization consultants, and trainers will find this edition helpful when leading, coaching, or training others.

The book is organized into four parts: Part I discusses evolving organizations today and the impact on teams and teamwork. Part II describes a facilitative style of leadership and introduces the L.E.A.D. model. Part III coaches readers in facilitating communication one on one and across distance teams. Part IV describes how to lead a productive team meeting and gives advice on planning a meeting, managing participation, working with group process, and helping a group to reach consensus.

PART ONE

Teamwork in Evolving Organizations

Today, in fast-paced, rapidly changing organizations, less gets done through hierarchical structures, and more is accomplished through small groups of people focused on a particular project or goal. We will look at the new workplace in Chapter One and examine its impact on teams and teamwork in Chapter Two.

1

The New Workplace

Many forces are shaping the workplace today, and organizations are in a constant state of evolution. Change is more frequent and pervasive than ever before. In fact, change is the only constant. We need a new word for this type of change, this change that has no beginning, no middle, and no end. We could call it "continuous fluctuation," or "expected turbulence," or "business flow." Whatever we call it, things change so quickly that businesses face everything they had to face in the past, only at triple and quadruple the speed!

Some things that occur faster or change more frequently than ever before are

- The life cycle of products (from inception to delivery)
- Communication methods and tools
- Delivery systems
- Decision making
- Formation and disbanding of teams
- Formation and disbanding of organizations
- Company mergers and acquisitions

- The rise of new products and services
- The employee makeup of an organization
- Organization goals and strategies
- Job requirements, positions, and the frequency with which people change jobs

Why does so much change so quickly? A quick look at the evolving world over recent years will help us to understand why business and organizations are so dynamic today.

The world of work has literally become "the world," as companies do business around the world and around the clock. Global, as well as local, factors must be considered in decisions, and people must be skilled at working across cultures and nationalities.

Technology has shortened the life cycle of products, made cross-global communication faster, proliferated information, created hundreds of new jobs, and left in its wake now obsolete methods, machinery, and knowledge. The once-familiar environments and boxes we called "jobs" do not exist in the way they did a decade ago. Industries have come and gone, or are waning, and new industries are on the horizon. The computer has changed the way we communicate, the way we do business, and the way people work together.

Technology has also created the twenty-four-hour clock. With the increased capability for communication via e-mail and the Internet, people today are expected to be in touch almost continually with those people important to the work they are doing. People all over the world can feasibly work around the clock, due to the ease and speed of today's communication and technology. As a result, workers may feel "married" to their work night and day, never totally free from the tug and demands of it.

More information is available to people, and it is available twenty-four hours a day. Employees have access to up-to-date company information via their company's intranet and to worldwide information via the Internet. Managers have less and less of a secretive hold on information, while employees have more information to do their jobs. Most people today have so much information that they hardly know where to begin to sift through it. Indeed, information management has become both a privilege and a challenge to everyone.

With all this change, job boundaries are blurred and job definitions outmoded. The nature of work today is that people move from project to project, from one organization structure to another, and from manager to manager. They may serve on several teams at once and "report" in a matrix fashion to multiple managers and team leaders.

Unemployment in the United States, especially for skilled and knowledgeable workers, is at an all-time low. Low unemployment means aggressive competition among organizations for qualified workers. It also means that people need to be motivated and treated well or they will seek work elsewhere. Low unemployment usually means more employee turnover.

The temperament of today's worker has also changed. Due to low unemployment, workers can demand more job benefits and special considerations. Workers want to be more and more independent, while the work they are doing calls for more and more connection. Younger workers are less patient with constraints and traditional approaches to work. Line and block chart reporting, bureaucratic complexities, close supervision, putting in a certain number of hours at work, wasting time in meetings, not being given authority to get work done, and waiting one's turn for development are not tolerated by today's competent, self-starting worker.

At one time, it was expected that everyone would hide his or her differences at work and melt into the workforce. People were expected to leave their ethnicity, backgrounds, gender, and creativity at home. Today, people expect to bring their identity to work with them and to make a meaningful contribution because of that identity. The world is diverse. The marketplace is diverse. The workplace is diverse.

Today's marketplace explodes with new products and services and is highly competitive, time-driven, and unpredictable. Companies with effective processes—meaning adaptable, responsive, action-oriented, risk-taking, and future-focused—will be poised to take advantage of new markets and trends. In fact, *the way a company works can determine whether or not it can stay in business*. Process is as critical as product! Some people say the process *is* the product. The only way to stay competitive is to use *processes* that ensure responsiveness to the marketplace. And because the marketplace is ever-changing, the processes too must change.

Managers at all levels are being forced to group and regroup, to think and rethink, not only the way they organize and run their organizations, but what their organizations are going to be about—not in the distant future—but tomorrow! The kind of collaboration, heads-together, innovative work that "work teams" were challenged with a decade ago is now in the laps of all leaders today. No one manager can make the complex decisions that arise in today's work environment. These decisions require team efforts, synergy, and the combined expertise of many.

Impact on Individuals

Individuals are impacted in many ways by the forces shaping the new workplace.

First, people no longer have jobs, they have assignments. They ①
may have a "job," but that job will change frequently. Actually,
they may have several assignments. They may serve on one fairly
stable team for as long as a year, or they may serve briefly on several teams, some with short and some with long lives. At a glance
from the air, the world of work may resemble a flowing river bob-
bing with little rowboats of "teams" with people jumping from one
boat to another.

Second, the roles of leaders and individuals continue to ②
change. Once-clear role boundaries are blurred today, and people
are often expected to do more than one job. They may be called
on to switch roles as needed to accomplish overall (and frequently
changing) goals of their organization. The formerly revered, one-
up/one-down manager-subordinate relationship has almost disap-
peared in today's high-growth, fast-paced organizations. Words
like "supervisor," "subordinate," "employee," and "manager" are
apt to be avoided, replaced by words such as "associate," "team
member," "team leader," or "colleague." Managers and their direct
reports are apt to work more as equals and teammates than as boss
and follower. The emphasis is on equalization of individuals at
work, implying that all aspects of work are important. If the work
is important enough to apply resources to it, then the person who
carries out that work is valuable. If all of the work is valuable, then
all of those who do the work are also valuable.

The role distinction between team leader and team member is
also diminishing. All people are expected to work on teams, sometimes several at once, and to work within hierarchical boundaries
when necessary, not against them. People frequently change hats
from team member to team leader to individual contributor to
manager to spokesperson. For some, this switching of roles occurs
on a regular basis. For others, it is occasional.

One person may serve in many capacities, such as team member, collaborator or partner, team leader, multi-team leader, or manager. People must become comfortable and adept at all aspects of teamwork: being on the team as a team member, directing the work of a team as a leader, coordinating and inspiring the work of several teams as a manager or multi-team leader.

Third, no one can know all he or she needs to know to do a job today. The individual worker is now in a similar dilemma to the manager of ten years ago—expected to carry out tasks and a role without enough knowledge, buy-in, or support. The individual worker of today must cull the wisdom and garner the support of other people to get the work done. The need, then, is to "team up," to understand when to "team," and then to know how to "team."

The exact team someone is on becomes less of an issue than how teamwork infuses much of what that person does. The person who refuses to team up—collaborate, share responsibility, share rewards—may be left without the information or support essential to do the job.

Fourth, skills that enable people to communicate openly (collaborate, innovate, decide, plan and develop methods for cohesive implementation of plans) are critical. Not only must people possess these skills, but also they must be able to use them quickly and adeptly in different environments. A person may represent his or her company at several facilities worldwide, be asked to travel globally and adjust to different cultures, and be expected to interact skillfully and in a timely manner with people of all levels and responsibilities, both within and without the organization. During any given week, this person may be operating in teamwork fashion with several different groups, departments, and even companies! In one setting this person may be presenting; in another listening; in another gathering information; and in yet another facilitating a meeting.

People need skills to facilitate numerous types of interchanges daily. Facilitation skills and the "listening" attitude that accompanies them are more and more important. With e-mail and the Internet, people communicate more often than ever before! How essential it is today to have the professional skills, not only of operating the machinery and protocols of electronic communication, but of using that communication to facilitate trust, clarify understandings, ask questions, and summarize—all skills required of a good facilitator.

Fifth, in today's workplace, people are expected to be "superworkers." They are expected to take initiative to not only do the work but, in many cases, to define it. They must define and redefine their role in light of organization goals and be less concerned with job title and description than they are with productively filling a gap in the organization.

Superworkers are expected to have necessary technical knowledge as well as the ability to communicate, influence, plan, organize, and garner support. They are asked to be team members as well as team leaders. They are expected both to observe the boundaries of their organization and to work around those boundaries in politically astute ways. They are encouraged to define their jobs broadly and be flexible with that definition. Those who do not show initiative to take on new assignments or who do not move flexibly throughout the organization to get things done are seen as not doing their jobs.

Sixth, everyone leads to some extent today, just to get the job done. They lead by sharing information, soliciting input, asking for support, obtaining data, building trust, suggesting solutions, making improvements, and taking an active role in meetings.

From Traditional to Team-Based Organizations

Over the past decade or so, organizations have shifted from traditional, hierarchical approaches to management to more team-based approaches. Many organizations have evolved from places in which employees were generally told what to do to places in which employees are involved in figuring out and deciding what they should do. Traditionally, managers hired, motivated, and directed the work of people who were assigned certain tasks to complete. In some cases teamwork was called for, but in many cases, individuals were given a job to do without the need to interact regularly with others. As jobs grew more complex, more specialists were needed. When a new job needed to be done, a new position was created and someone was hired to fill that position.

In general, people worked apart from one another, coming together only to inform one another or to solve a problem pertaining to the whole group. The work of the group as a whole was overseen and directed by the manager.

Several "old paradigms" (patterns and practices) justified managing people this way:

- The manager was the technical expert.
- The manager made final decisions.
- The manager used a directive, decisive style.
- The manager imposed controls on employees.
- The manager defined how work got done.
- The manager processed all information and communicated it to employees.
- The manager developed the group's goals.
- The manager administered rewards and punishments.

- Employees needed only a few skills to do their jobs.
- The focus was on specialization.
- The organization was concerned mainly with its own purpose.
- Manager-employee relationships were based on a "we" and "they" distinction.
- People operated within narrow job definitions.
- The organization was structured hierarchically.
- Teams were formed when needed.
- The workforce was homogeneous.
- Change was the exception, not the rule.

Much has happened to dramatize the limitations of these old paradigms. Managers have not been able to keep up with technical advances and new information. Therefore, their former role as experts has become outdated, and they must now rely heavily on technical experts for help in making decisions. In fact, managers can no longer even be expected to set the group's goals single-handedly.

The old paradigms defined individuals' roles narrowly. The strong focus on specialization and the narrow definition of people's jobs made it almost impossible to solve problems that involved several jobs, functions, departments, or, in many cases, divisions or even companies. Too many problems fell between the cracks—between jobs or functions—and no one was there to solve them. An over-focus on specialization led to the attitude expressed in "That's not my job," a problem that caused vast inefficiencies in business.

When managers and their people set up "we-they" boundaries, the result was more adversarial than cooperative. The old paradigms created tension, which often caused management and employees to counter each other. The old paradigms placed a great deal of emphasis on doing the task without addressing the important social dimension of teamwork and organizational work life. Older methods therefore often failed to gain enough commitment from employees to get the job done.

Many new paradigms have worked their way into organizations because of the climate in which today's companies operate. Organizations have implemented new approaches, focusing on greater involvement of employees in decision making and planning, with varying degrees of success. Nonetheless, these new paradigms have evolved and are still evolving:

- Employees are experts possessing unique technical knowledge and skills.
- Employees are the natural ones to make some decisions.
- Controls are minimized or set collectively.
- Employees participate in defining how work is done.
- Employees participate in setting and interpreting group goals.
- People are resources to be developed and used fully.
- Jobs are defined broadly and require multiple skills.
- Employees focus on applying special knowledge to larger problems.
- The organization is concerned with members' and society's purposes as well as its own.
- "Partnership" relationships are fostered between managers and employees.
- Teamwork is structured into the organization.

- Creative and productive outcomes result from the synergy of teamwork.

- Teams take over some of the work of managers.

- Organization structures are flatter.

- People are given larger boundaries and encouraged to develop more skills.

- The organization is customer/market driven.

- The workforce is diverse.

- Change is the norm.

Under the old paradigms, employees had few decisions to make and relied heavily on the manager to direct their work. Under the new paradigms, employees take on more responsibility, moving into areas once reserved for management. Just as management's role changes in participative companies, so does the role of employees.

Teamwork Addresses Old Paradigm Problems

Effective teamwork addresses two key problems with the old paradigms. First, under the old paradigms, the talents of individual employees were often not fully used, and the organization suffered as a result. Second, the isolation of individuals meant that organizations failed to capitalize on *synergy*, the effect of working to achieve something collectively that could not have been achieved through individual efforts. The output of group work is, in many instances, greater than the combined output of its individual members working alone.

Organizations realize that allowing people to consistently work alone does not yield the return on investment the organization needs to succeed in today's competitive marketplace. Because of the complexity of today's business problems and the continual change faced by organizations, the resources of all employees must be available when appropriate and necessary. Leaders must be able to rely on the wisdom of the group to solve not just the occasional mind-boggling problem but also the ongoing, day-to-day concerns faced by every organization.

Summary

Today's workplace is characterized by change, blurred boundaries, temporary systems, a proliferation of information, a global arena, and people who want more from their jobs than ever before. Philosophies and values may remain for years, but markets, products, processes, and physical locations change again and again. To respond to such rapidly changing environments, organizations must be flexible, innovate, use employees effectively, and be vitally aware of the dynamics in the world around them.

2

From Teams to Teamwork

Today's organizations are more like webs than line and box structures. Even though official leadership channels may exist as line and box structures, real work happens much more organically. Any collection of people working on the same project or goals must, whether formally or informally, act as a team. But it must work more efficiently and be more focused than ever before. A team can get very little done by itself and must link and network outside itself to understand, plan, and carry out its work. Quickly formed teams, ad hoc teams, partnerships, and continually modulated organizational structures keep individuals networking within these webs. Everyone is on one or more teams; each person may in turn have to form, lead, or serve on a team, at least some of the time, to get work done.

Definitions of Team and Teamwork

A workable definition of a *team* is "two or more people who work collaboratively to make something happen." With this definition in mind, think of all the teams people are on! Whenever someone teams up with someone else to agree on an action, they are, for those moments in time, a "team."

Teamwork is "the act of two or more people working collaboratively to make something happen." To succeed in organizations today, people need to "team" a lot. The spirit of teamwork must infuse much of what people do at work—not all of it, but much of it. You may not call the group of people you work with a team. No one else may call it a team. But the way the work needs to get done will often be through teamwork.

The Purpose of Teams

Generally speaking, the *purpose* of a team is to accomplish one or more necessary tasks or responsibilities that cannot be accomplished by individuals working alone. The *focus* of a team is to get work done that supports the goals of the organization. If an organization is small, everyone in it may be part of the organization team. This doesn't mean that all the work will be done as a team. What it means is that whenever there is work to be done that requires the collaborative effort of more than one person, the team comes into play. Of course, there are always gray areas. Who's to say what requires teamwork and what doesn't? There may be disagreement here. However, there are generally plenty of opportunities in organizations for which teamwork is essential or desirable.

Teamwork in Evolving Organizations

In the 1980s and early 1990s, efforts were focused on "work teams," those teams that fell into the lower and middle levels of the organization. Higher level managers and leaders wanted teamwork to happen at this level partly because it served the purposes of downsizing and of increasing productivity with fewer people. Managers realized the importance of teamwork for the sake of quality and implementation of plans. However, this same level of teamwork seldom happened at the top. At the top, organizations for the most part stayed fixed in their hierarchies and functional arenas. They were less skilled at facilitating: listening, collaborating, obtaining support for decisions, using consensus processes, and leading participative meetings. They continued with their traditional managerial duties of directing, influencing, persuading, approving, organizing, and doling out performance rewards.

Moving into the 21st Century, many dynamic and successful organizations encourage and model teamwork across all levels of the organization. What were once traditional management duties are more apt to be shared among teams, team leaders, and superworkers. What drives organizations today are the current goals and the immediate work: what needs to be done, who can do it, and when it must be accomplished. Teams are vital to this process. They can be quickly formed for specific tasks or projects and then disbanded or restructured to meet the next need.

Rather than restructure with each change in the business, organizations rely on marshaling groups of people more informally to make things happen, from the initial idea and planning stages through implementation and evaluation. Organizations cannot afford to take the time to pass off plans from one function to another. Frequently, all functions, levels, divisions, and even resources outside the organization must come together to determine the goals and next steps, and then they must operate in parallel, communicating all along the way. This, of course, requires teamwork and all that goes with it: face-to-face communication, involvement, the right team members, a team-oriented process, and qualified, skillful team leadership.

Leaders must work with people to create temporary boundaries, the ones that will ensure the work gets done, when it must get done. This means frequent meetings (yes, more meetings!), clarifying outputs and goals, open discussions, creative sessions, coming to consensus, shared responsibility, and listening to others. There must be a willingness on everyone's part to make getting the work done more important than what job they have, what team they're on, and whether or not they are the team leader. Teamwork and facilitation skills are not the end, but the means to the end. If the process doesn't work, the work won't get done.

Although hierarchies are still in place in many organizations, responsibilities, titles, and positions change so rapidly that structure means less than it did ten and twenty years ago. Because changes happen faster, teamwork is required from start to finish, and this teamwork is generally across functions and boundaries from start to finish.

Teamwork as Spirit

The spirit of teamwork is more important today than the designation, selection, and managing of "teams" per se. The organization is a team; the question is, *How good a team?* Effective teamwork is required of all players—employees, leaders, vendors, suppliers, customers, regulators, the community—all are important to doing business in a dynamic world. Those who lead today—and indeed, certain levels of leadership are required of everyone—must have basic teamwork skills to make things happen.

Teams were initially formed to help individuals who worked together function optimally. Now teamwork is needed not only for team member interaction but also from team to team, across departments, and outside one's organization as well. Teams form throughout the organization as the work demands. Team leaders are somewhat like short-order cooks: take the order, cook it, serve it up, and then move on to the next assignment. People flow in and out of teams as needed. They may function in one capacity as a manager of a group of people (each of whom may sit on several teams), in another capacity as a team leader, and still another capacity as a team member. The entire organization can be likened to a collection of floating, ever-changing teams, with individuals moving in and out of these teams on a regular basis.

Teams are the structure; teamwork is the process. Teams are ways to organize. Teamwork is the way a person thinks and works. Teamwork is more than skills. It is more than structure. It is more than forced group cooperation. Teamwork, at its best, is a spirit, the spirit of cooperation fueled with the desire to excel. Teamwork is both an individual process and an organizational process. For it to really work, it must be infused into the daily operations of an organization.

Teamwork and the Distribution of Power

Today, as we enter the 21st Century, it is not an issue of *whether* we "empower" employees by letting them share the responsibilities of planning and decision making; it is an issue of *how well* we do this, *because we must!* Organizations need employees who share responsibility, who become engaged with work in a creative, dedicated way. Involved employees—those who think with and for the company, who instigate teamwork on their own, who take an active role in engineering the changes their organizations must make— are critical to today's organizations. With the current trend to do more with fewer people, employees are overloaded and management stretched to the limit. There is no room to waste employee time or to have teams functioning poorly. To do more with less, organizations also have to do better with less: better communication, better leadership, better teamwork, and better utilization of people.

Historically, leadership and power were concentrated in a few individuals. Decision authority rested in one or two key people in an organization, who were rewarded (or punished) for the quality of their decisions. Because of the complexity of information required to make an intelligent decision quickly, the chance that one person will make that decision effectively is diminished. The organization loses the benefit that a diverse, broad spectrum of input provides. Organizations that ignore team efforts and rely on autocratic decision making by a few managers will eventually fail because one person cannot make the best decisions all the time.

To make things happen quickly, efficiently, and in a quality manner, people must meet and talk frequently with one another and come up with sound ways to proceed. Without this kind of teamwork, we are back to the "old-fashioned" way of managing: manager knows all, directs and motivates his or her subordinates, and maneuvers the work through motivation or coercion of these subordinates. Manager takes full responsibility for the work on his or her shoulders. Subordinates find their niche, the piece of work they will and can do, and refuse to cooperate with one another. The manager acts as mediator between individuals. In contrast, in a teamwork environment, the manager becomes a team leader, facilitating the team members to determine how they will support overall organization goals.

Teamwork as an Investment

Teamwork is an investment and takes a long-term approach and commitment. In today's instant decision environment, teamwork is often sacrificed for speed. There is so much competition, so much pressure, and so much change. It is understandable that leaders might revert to directive, autocratic styles of leadership. It takes courage and foresight to work collaboratively. Time and planning are needed to build teams, to include people in critical decisions, and to allow risk taking.

A team can

- Provide ideas
- Provide a sanity check for decisions
- Filter logic through a variety of perspectives
- Slow down an overly quick decision process
- Provide valuable information
- Ensure commitment, which will facilitate implementing the decision
- Provide support for the vision and goals
- Come up with a quality decision
- Help review and digest contradictions in a decision

Skirting teamwork may work for some short-term fixes. But in the long run, lack of teamwork makes a company vulnerable because it isn't building unity and cooperation. It isn't <u>utilizing its people's best talents</u>. It isn't getting buy-in. It isn't keeping people <u>motivated to be there and contribute</u>. Instead, it is continually pulling uphill.

Even though it is difficult to do in fast-paced, changeable organizations, it behooves organizations to build atmospheres in which teamwork flourishes. Over time, there are many benefits. Here are some:

- People are motivated to contribute their knowledge and creativity.
- Buy-in occurs up front.
- Complex decisions are made with adequate technical and nontechnical information.
- No one person is expected to make all the decisions.

- Those who know the most about the work have an active say in how the work is done.

- People, as a critical and expensive resource, are developed and used fully.

- "Partnership" relations are encouraged between managers and employees.

- All people are more likely to be valued, which increases the likelihood that people will contribute in valuable ways.

- Teamwork takes advantage of possible synergies.

- People are encouraged to develop more skills, and the organization benefits.

- Change is dealt with more efficiently when people are involved in planning and navigating the change.

- Responsibility is shared throughout the organization, not dropped into the laps of a few.

Given the challenges facing team leaders today, it is understandable that teamwork often flies in the face of pressure. However, given the long-term benefits of teamwork and of building effective teams, organization will do well to support team leaders and teams in their efforts to improve performance through teamwork.

Teamwork as a Motivator

When there is low unemployment, people have more choices about which organization to join. If you don't value your workforce, they will not value the work they do for you, and they will go where they are valued and where they can value the work they do. There are no perfect decisions, so involving people in making them—especially when this is much more likely to motivate and retain good people—is an effective strategy. In addition, statistics show that groups consistently make better quality, more creative decisions than individuals alone.

When people feel valued in an organization, they are more apt to respond positively to teamwork. Leaders will not get quality information from a team of people unless they value those people for their decision-making ability. If people are asked for input and if they truly believe that input will be taken seriously, they will be more likely to contribute honest, quality information. However, if they sense that the attitude of the leader is "Go ahead and tell me what you think, but I'm not really going to use that information. I'm going to take that information and work it over with a smaller group of people that I trust," they are likely to shut down.

The more at ease an organization's employees are with teamwork and collaboration, the more capable the organization is to move decisions and actions through the organization to completion. An atmosphere of teamwork and collaboration encourages more productive interactions with customers and the acquiring of information from many and varied sources. Team members who are skilled at facilitation and group process can marshal forces to move forward more effectively and with more coordination than members who are dependent on leaders to bring them to collaboration. For example, salespeople who deal continually with customers can use their facilitation skills to lead company/customer meetings, come to agreement on contracts, and represent the customer in the context of their own organizations. Facilitation skills are not only critical for team leaders, they are *essential* for all leaders, as well as team members and individual contributors.

Teams Working with Teams

A team seldom operates alone. Multiple teams must work in concert, and this means teamwork across team boundaries as well. Teams not only have to be skilled at doing their work (and this sometimes includes figuring out what that work is), but they must also be able to know when to contact and involve other teams, how to hand off their work, how not to foul up another team's work, and how to keep redundancies to a minimum. This requires cross-team communication and cooperation. Some cases require "linking teams," those teams comprising members from several teams who make sure the work of several teams is coordinated.

Of course, not all work requires collaborative efforts from beginning to end. Just as important as good team leadership is leadership that knows when *not* to assign a task to a team. However, even when individuals are assigned independent work, there is often a team component to some of their work. Independent workers can benefit by approaching others with a spirit of teamwork, people from whom they must obtain information, ideas, or support. The person who assigns work and the person who carries out the work become a team of two. They must collaborate at least in defining and negotiating what the work is, and certainly a spirit of teamwork will help get the work off to a good start—and finish. Whether work is assigned to a team or an individual, there will be a teamwork component somewhere. Good leaders know how to coach and encourage their independent workers to align themselves with others, in at least a spirit of teamwork, to get work done. They may not have to collaborate to get the work done, but some collaboration will likely help the finished product to support the work of others and the goals of the organization.

Summary

Teamwork is very much a part of work today. How it's done may look a bit different than it did ten years ago, but it is still teamwork. Even with all the change organizations face today, each person's work is still connected to another's. Functions must work in concert with other functions, and organizations must work in coordination with their counterparts, customers, suppliers, and regulators. These connections call for teamwork on every front. People must communicate, collaborate, pass work along, fill in for others, make group decisions, brainstorm, and problem solve together.

The nature of work today is such that teamwork is required to decide what the work is, determine how it should be approached, and discover how to survive under the challenges of the marketplace. Teamwork takes place one-on-one, among colleagues, between managers and their direct reports, between departments, across organizational boundaries, and within small work groups. Teamwork is more than skills; it is more than structure; it is more than forced group consensus. Teamwork is a *process*; it is the very way people approach work. And in today's work environment, everyone may need to take a team or facilitative leadership role from time to time.

PART TWO

A Facilitative Style of Leadership

Leading teams calls for a different style of leadership than does managing in hierarchical organizations. In hierarchical organizations, decision making is typically the domain of management, which in turn delegates jobs and tasks to individuals. The role of a traditional manager is one of decision maker, delegator, presenter, and coach. In team-oriented organizations, a facilitative style of leadership is more effective. This style of leadership focuses on motivating and involving others to set and accomplish goals synergistically. Decisions are made more by consensus and collaboration. The role of a team leader is the one of coach, motivator, team member, and facilitator.

Chapter Three provides an introduction to the L.E.A.D. model of leadership and ten essentials of teamwork. In Chapter Four leadership styles are explained on a continuum from controlling to facilitating and leaders are encouraged to gain skills in leading from a facilitative approach, because controlling and directive approaches are often not as productive in today's teamwork-oriented cultures. Chapter Five contains a discussion of facilitation in relation to sparking team spirit and accomplishing work in teams, and Chapter Six is a description of the new team leader in today's organizations.

3

How to L.E.A.D.

Leading teamwork is an effort to get people to work synergistically and productively together. The leadership role required to lead a team can be described in a simple, four-point model, the L.E.A.D. model. This model indicates four goals that a facilitative leader keeps in mind at all times:

- **L**ead with a clear purpose
- **E**mpower to participate
- **A**im for consensus
- **D**irect the process

The model will be explained in detail later in this chapter. Before discussing the model, it helps to review and understand basic conditions that must be in place for people to work well in a team. When the L.E.A.D. model is in action, ten essentials of teamwork can be realized.

Ten Essentials of Teamwork

What makes a collection of people become a team? What keeps team members working well together? What do groups need to function productively? If a team is defined as two or more people working collaboratively to make something happen, then team members have mutually interdependent purposes. The success of one team member is contingent on the success of others. In addition, each person has a sense of belonging or membership, and all team members accept certain behaviors based on group norms, procedures, and constraints.

Studies in group dynamics (what goes on among people in group settings) show that teams or groups have certain key needs (see Figure 3.1, Key Needs of Teams). For a team to stay alive and function well, the following needs must be met:

Common Goals. Members of a team need a reason for being and working together. The goals of a team rationalize its existence. Although the goals may change over time, each member should clearly understand what these goals are at any point. The less clear the goals are, the more likely it is that they will be misinterpreted by team members and the more likely it is that the group will suffer internal tensions, argue, and work at cross-purposes. Without clear goals, people become apathetic or use the group to achieve their own personal goals.

Leadership. Teams need leaders and members who can lead when necessary. Whether a group has a formal leader or leadership is shared, the group needs people who are willing to take the risk of leadership. Leaders are the people who are respected and influential enough to get others to try team-oriented approaches to working together, obtain support from reluctant members, and build bridges with groups and people outside the team. Leaders help coordinate the work of the team, have good communication skills, and know how to involve everyone.

FIGURE 3.1. Key Needs of Teams.

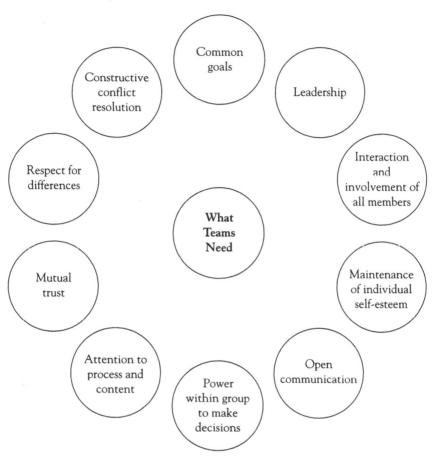

Interaction and Involvement of All Members. To achieve synergy and group spirit, all team members must contribute actively. Holding back creates problems for the team. Therefore, it is important for team leaders to know how to get everyone involved.

Maintenance of Individual Self-Esteem. The good of the group should not prevail to the point that members lose self-esteem. Each person's contribution must be heard, valued, and acknowledged. Favoritism must be avoided, and members must be encouraged to be themselves. The challenge to the team and to the leader is to enhance, not lower, the self-esteem of each member.

Open Communication. Team members need to feel that they can speak their minds, that the channels of communication are open to everyone, especially to the leader. The team should have ample time to communicate; share information; discuss issues; and use informal communication channels to pass on information, make suggestions, and bring up new ideas.

Power Within the Group to Make Decisions. The work of the team should center around the things it has the power to influence. Giving teams work to do that is not approved for implementation is unproductive and demotivating. Some of the failure of early quality circles in the United States can be traced to the fact that the suggestions they made were sometimes either ignored or vetoed higher up. These teams were not given the power to carry out the work they were asked to do. If more decisions were made at the level where they were carried out, people would have more reasons to work together in teams.

Attention to Both Process and Content. For people to function well together as a group, attention must be paid both to the process used to do the work and to the content of the work or the group's task. Process includes attention to how people get along together, how the work is structured and distributed, and what the general rules of working together are. Usually, the task to be done receives a lot of attention, while the process of how the team members work together is expected to fall into place. Because process problems may hurt feelings and impede progress, it is best to address the team's process, along with its tasks.

Mutual Trust. Trust depends on how the leader and members treat one another. When something happens to break that trust (a commitment not met, a confidentiality betrayed, dishonesty), it can be difficult to retrieve. Members and the team leader may need to discuss how their behaviors and attitudes affect trust. Then everyone will have to try to do those things that will build and maintain trust.

Respect for Differences. Team members must feel they can disagree and differ from one another without being punished. The leader sets the tone, but each member has to take responsibility for acknowledging and respecting the needs of others. When individuals on a team are not getting some of their needs met, teamwork becomes demotivating for them.

Constructive Conflict Resolution. Conflict is natural. When it surfaces, it must be addressed in a healthy way. Again, the leader plays an important role in helping group members to express conflict and come to general agreement. Unresolved conflict leads to less-than-adequate performance, resentments, and lack of motivation.

Task and Social Dimensions of Teamwork

Teamwork has two dimensions: task and social. These two dimensions are inseparable, for without either, teamwork does not exist. Effective team leaders work continually with both dimensions, as must team members themselves. The task dimension refers to the work that team members are to perform—the jobs they have to do and how they are going to do those jobs. The social dimension refers to how team members feel toward one another and their membership on the team. At any given point in the team's work, both the task and social dimensions operate. When team members make a decision and develop ideas, they are simultaneously developing ways to get along together. To the extent the team does its tasks well, it will be productive. To the extent it manages its relationships well, team members will have a sense of belonging and commitment.

Preserving the Dignity of the Individual

Leaders will do well to think of a team as a collection of diverse individuals, each with his or her own unique character and potential for contribution to the group. Being expected to conform and to subjugate individual needs and desires for the common good is degrading to team members. The fact is that some people are more comfortable as part of a group than others. Some more independent members may feel constrained and ill at ease working in a team. Others, because of their race, gender, age, religion, or culture, may not have much in common with other members and yet feel pressured to get along and conform. An effective leader is sensitive to the need to preserve individual dignity, to capitalize on differences, and to not try to achieve conformity.

Over the years, teamwork has acquired a bad reputation, and one of the key reasons is that many people fear being "swallowed up" by the team. They fear losing personal power and identity. They lack patience to work with others and would rather be working independently. They are frustrated with taking time for the team to reach consensus, and they want to make their own personal mark on their work. As a result, people often subtly and not so subtly resist teamwork.

An effective team leader realizes the need for individuality and builds this into teamwork. A good facilitative leader views teamwork as an ongoing negotiation among diverse individuals who are setting and working toward common goals. The skills of facilitation help leaders blend different views into consensus so the team can achieve its goals. The effective team leader acknowledges individual differences and challenges the team to meet as many individual needs as possible while achieving the team's goals. Team leaders and team members can work together to give individuals the opportunity to work both alone and with others. Individual members can still be recognized and encouraged to put their mark on the work. When this is done in conjunction with the whole efforts and buy-in of the team, everyone benefits.

The L.E.A.D. Model of Leadership

Using a simple four-step model when leading will increase the chances that the ten essentials of teamwork will be addressed and that team member participation will be healthy and productive:

- **L**ead with a clear purpose
- **E**mpower to participate
- **A**im for consensus
- **D**irect the process

The L.E.A.D. model includes key leadership functions: setting clear goals and objectives, involving people, reaching consensus on important items, and paying attention to both tasks (the work) and relationships (the team). Following this model ensures that the ten essentials of teamwork are met and provides the *leadership* that any team needs. Leading with a clear purpose meets the need for *common goals*. Empowering members to participate achieves the high level of *interaction and involvement* that group members need. Participation and consensus help maintain *individual self-esteem* and encourage *open communication*. Participation and consensus also help build *mutual trust* and achieve a healthy *respect for differences among team members*, while providing an avenue for *constructive conflict resolution*. Using all four parts of the model will assure that there is *power within the group to make decisions*. Leading with a clear purpose and directing the process ensure that leaders pay *attention to both process and content*.

The following paragraphs offer a more detailed analysis of the L.E.A.D. model.

Lead with a Clear Purpose

To lead with a clear purpose simply means to use goals as a motivator for teams. For goals to motivate people, they need to be challenging, positive, and realistic. A leader can give power and focus to the team's goals in several ways.

First, set realistic, team-oriented goals that tie to the company's goals. Team-oriented goals are ones that apply specifically to your team. They are the things your team needs to accomplish to support the larger company goals. The company's goals are not immediate enough to motivate your team. You must help your team identify specific goals that it alone can accomplish. Make sure they support the company goals.

Next, publish those goals. Make them visible for all to see. Do not expect people to remember them if they are not discussed and referred to often. Do not bury them in occasional memos and documents. Instead, post them in meeting rooms on flip charts or posters; use stickers or other visual reminders to keep the goals in front of everyone. Refer to the goals often in memos, presentations, and meetings. Whenever possible, use the goals to guide a decision. Ask others to do the same. When someone comes to you with a problem or suggestion, say something like, "In light of our goal of 95 percent on-time deliveries, what do you think is the best solution?"

Work with your team to identify milestones that will show you are making progress toward your goals. Keep these subgoals in front of your people, with deadlines whenever possible. For example, you might have these milestones for the goal of achieving 95 percent on-time delivery:

- 85 percent by the end of the third quarter
- 90 percent by the end of the fourth quarter
- 93 percent by the end of the first quarter of next year
- 95 percent by the end of the second quarter of next year

Track and report the team's progress in achieving its established goals. When a milestone is achieved, acknowledge it and celebrate it. Take a little time out to feel good about meeting a goal. Over time, allow your team to set its own goals, monitor its own progress, and plan its own celebrations.

Empower to Participate

Once goals have been established and published, your next step is to empower people to participate in achieving those goals. The word "empower" means to give power or authority, to authorize, to enable or permit. Thus, it means you can begin to facilitate, to help others to determine how goals will be achieved. Even though the goals themselves may motivate the team, team members become unmotivated if they cannot participate in important decisions regarding ways to achieve those goals—especially if they are expected to carry out those decisions.

Not everyone needs to participate in every decision, but people should participate in those decisions they will have to implement. "Who will we depend on to carry out this decision?" is the key question here. Those people should at least be consulted about the decision that is made. Some decisions may naturally fall to one or two team members. Others will need to be made by the entire team. Still others may require the representation of others outside the team.

As a leader, you have at least two choices when it comes to involving your team in making a decision. One is simply to consult with team members and then make the decision yourself. Alternatively, you can work with others (one, a few, or the whole group) to come to a consensus about the decision. When a consensus decision is made, you have the option of remaining neutral and simply facilitating the decision process or becoming a member of the group making the decision. The role you choose depends on several factors, such as your comfort with letting the group decide, your ability to avoid over-influencing the group's decision, how much you have to be involved in implementation, and whether team members want your involvement.

You have many other ways to empower people to participate. You can, of course, involve the team in setting its own goals. You may decide to redesign jobs and procedures so team members will have to interact to do the work. You can identify which types of decisions you will make and which types of decisions the team or team members will make.

One of the main principles of facilitation is to help others to solve problems they are capable of solving. You can encourage more involvement by learning techniques to help others to solve their own problems. These techniques are covered in later chapters: Chapter Seven deals with getting someone to solve his or her own problems; Chapters Nine through Fourteen deal with helping groups to solve problems on their own.

Facilitative leaders encourage participation by listening more than talking and by asking more than telling. Two skills are therefore critical for good facilitators: _listening_ and _asking questions_. Listening, or _active listening,_ is required to hear, really hear, what the other person is saying. Active listening requires that you observe the other person as well as hear his or her words. The other person's body language, tone of voice, eye contact, and other signals will give you additional information about how that person perceives the issue. Active listening requires that your own body language indicate your receptiveness to the other person; maintain an open posture, nod your head, be still, keep eye contact—all these and more show that you are paying attention. Active listening also means not being distracted by others, by the surrounding environment, or by difficulties the speaker may have in putting his or her message across. It means not thinking about what you are going to say while the other person is talking. It also means that instead of jumping ahead to judge the other person or figure out why his or her remarks are not valid, you must postpone judgment until you have heard that person out.

Unfortunately, sometimes we are a bit lazy or too preoccupied to listen. We may be pressured with other issues. We may be feeling down or defensive or have a hard time being patient while the other person talks. We may wish we were somewhere else. Or we may misunderstand the other person. Here is where another aspect of active listening comes into play. In addition to knowing how to listen, we must know when to ask questions or clarify what the other person has been saying. We can repeat a brief version of what we thought was said, or _paraphrase,_ to check out the accuracy of our interpretation. Or we may ask the person to give us more

*active listening

ask for

more information or help clear up our confusion. Generally, it is best to give the other person a chance to talk, to formulate his or her thoughts, and to finish what he or she wants to say before jumping in with questions. Such patience is a rare commodity in a busy, pressured, rapidly changing world; but it is nonetheless a highly important trait for good listeners—and especially for good leaders.

Another way to empower team members is to regularly seek their ideas, opinions, and reactions without judging or punishing them for what they say. This is in fact a very simple habit to get into, but it is often overlooked. Leaders are often busy people, and some do not have a lot of opportunity to interact with their people. A good leader-facilitator, however, will make time to seek others' opinions and ideas, even if only for a few minutes in the hall. Stopping by a person's office for the sole purpose of asking for his or her opinion is particularly empowering for that person. You might say something like: "Jan, I'm interested in your opinion of the Blair account. What do you think we should do to improve that situation?"

Once you have asked someone else's opinion, the next few steps are critical. You must

1. Listen actively
2. Ask questions or paraphrase to clarify what was said
3. Thank the person, and *resist having the last word*

Sometimes you will be tempted to offer your opinion (especially if the other person asks for it). One of the best ways you can empower others to speak up is to listen without having the final word. Staying neutral for a while frees others to express their true opinions. Because you are the leader, your opinion can sway others. If you really want to hear what others think, let them talk without trying to influence them or being defensive.

Avoid letting others rely on you for answers. Instead, when someone comes to you for an answer or decision, ask what he or she thinks. Using this technique does not mean that you do not have an opinion or that you are abdicating your leadership role. It means you are encouraging others to solve their own problems. You are giving them permission— empowering them—to take on some of the leadership role.

Leaders who encourage their teams to make decisions must then support those decisions. If you must help implement the decision, then you should be involved in the decision-making process along with everyone else. But even if you do not need to be involved, you still must support your team once the decision is made. Support comes in many forms: having a positive attitude, offering your assistance, running interference, explaining to your superiors what your team is doing, and giving encouragement.

To encourage participation, give the team regular opportunities (probably at team meetings) to assess itself. You are not the only one to measure the team's performance. Teach the team members how to measure its own performance. When assessing itself, the team should cover both how well it is achieving its goals and how well it is doing as a team. Are good relationships being built among team members? Is there a spirit of cooperation? Are members working out differences in acceptable ways? What team norms (ground rules) are working? What norms need to be changed or added?

Finally, become proficient at giving genuinely positive reinforcement to your team members. Watch for things they are doing well, and let them know that you appreciate what they have done. Here are some general principles to follow when giving praise:

- Be specific about what you are praising
- Be timely; do not wait too long after the event or behavior

- Keep the praise separate from problems or negative concerns; it may be lost if it is sandwiched between problems

- Give praise regularly but not so often that it becomes expected or meaningless

Leaders who pay attention to their team members—listen to what they have to say, show interest in their concerns, take action when possible to alleviate difficulties, recognize them for a job well done, encourage them to grow and try new things, and offer guidance when they are unsure—develop more motivated teams. This level of caring and coaching is frequently missing from leaders and managers. Yet, frequently, this is what people are yearning for: consideration, attention, and encouragement. The role of a team leader becomes the role of coach, nurturer, fan, and resource provider.

Aim for Consensus

The third step in the L.E.A.D. model, aim for consensus, means helping people move toward general agreement. Foster consensus throughout the process of working with others, not just as a final step. Expect conflicts, but treat them as natural and work through them. Your role in building consensus is to bring as many ideas, opinions, and conflicts to the surface as possible and then to help people find the approach that best meets the needs of the organization and individual team members. For example, an organization goal may be to decrease delivery lead times, while individuals may not want to work longer hours to make that happen. During discussions, it is discovered that if individuals received more timely information, the delivery lead times goal could be met without having to make people work longer hours. Instead of simply pushing on people to meet the goal, the organization does its part to help individuals, and there is a win for both. This win-win solution is discovered while involving people in the decision.

After gaining general agreement, it is your responsibility as a leader to act on the decision or to empower the group to act on it. You may use the group's input to make a decision yourself, or you may let the group's decision stand.

Direct the Process

The last step in the L.E.A.D. model, direct the process, requires experience in working with groups and knowledge about the group process. An effective team leader will use various techniques, many discussed in the following chapters, to help the team complete its work. The process is how the team members work together and is separate from the actual content of decisions, plans, and actions.

How a team works together includes such things as how team members behave in team meetings, how communication occurs, what approaches the team takes to resolve problems and conflicts, how team members treat one another, and how the team leader and members relate to one another. Process relates to all of the dynamics of the team's working together, including the organization culture in which the team operates. It includes anything that impacts how the team works or how the team develops over time.

The facilitative leader takes responsibility for overseeing how the process of teamwork is progressing and makes suggestions to the team accordingly. To "direct the process" does not mean to order the team about in a directive manner; it means to guide the team by suggesting ways to structure the team's work so that team members, the team as a whole, and the organization benefit as much as possible. To direct the process means to be aware of methods and practices that help team members work well together. It means knowing how to explain the purpose of approaches and methods to the team. It means knowing when to ask the team for feedback on methods and knowing when to ask the team how it wants to proceed.

Here is a quick process checklist to determine whether there are process problems on a team:

- Is everyone participating?
- Are the right people involved on the team and present at team meetings?
- Are members communicating well with one another (in team meetings, via telephone, e-mail, and so forth)?
- Are members free to disagree with one another?
- Are members working through differences of opinion, or are they stymied by them?
- Are there interpersonal conflicts on the team?
- Does the team have healthy team norms or guidelines for behavior that all members have bought into and, preferably, that all members have helped develop?
- Do team members follow the norms?
- Are the goals of the team clear to everyone on the team? How do you know this?
- Is the mission and/or goal of the team written down, and does every member have a copy?
- Do team members take an active part in deciding ways to improve the functioning of the team?

- Are you, the team leader, comfortable with facilitating the team? Is responsibility for the team's success shared by all?

- Do team members take responsibility for attending team meetings and for completing agreed on action items?

- Is the team making progress on its tasks and goals?

- Is the team making progress on how well members work together?

- Do members have a sense that they belong to the team?

- Is it clear who is on, and who is not on, the team? Does it matter?

As a facilitative team leader, it pays to become skilled at observing group process, that is, how the group is working together. Once you see a problem, you can then suggest a process for helping correct it. Just because you are the team's leader doesn't mean you have full responsibility for correcting how the team works together. You are helping the team come up with ways to improve how it functions as a team. If you facilitate the team to come up with its own solutions, team members will be more apt to support what was decided.

Summary

Figure 3.2, Using the L.E.A.D. Model, lists the important group needs met in each point of the model and lists key tasks that must be performed by the leader and by team members. The L.E.A.D. model provides ample opportunity for employees to take part in the management of their organizations and gives leaders a critical role to play in making this happen.

FIGURE 3.2. Using the L.E.A.D. Model.

Leader Functions	Group Needs Met	Leader Tasks	Team Member Tasks
Lead with a clear purpose	• Common goals • Attention to content • Leadership	• Set boundaries • Interpret company goals • Facilitate team's setting of its own goals • Evaluate and track progress toward goals	• Ask questions to test own understanding • Participate in setting goals for team • Help leader track and evaluate progress toward goals
Empower to participate	• High level of involvement of all members • Maintenance of self-esteem • Leadership • Respect for differences • Trust	• Ask questions • Listen • Show understanding • Summarize • Seek divergent viewpoints • Record ideas	• Contribute ideas from own experience and knowledge • Listen to others • Build on ideas of others • Consider ideas of others • Ask questions • Think creatively

Leader Functions	Group Needs Met	Leader Tasks	Team Member Tasks
Aim for consensus	• Constructive conflict resolution • Power within groups to make decisions • Leadership • Trust	• Use group-process techniques (brainstorming, problem solving, prioritization, etc.) • Ask questions • Listen • Seek common interests • Summarize • Confront in constructive way	• Focus on common interests and goals • Listen to and consider ideas of others • Make own needs known • Disagree in constructive way
Direct the process	• Attention to process • Leadership • Trust	• Give clear directions • Intervene to keep group on track • Read group and adjust • Remain neutral • Suggest alternate processes to help group achieve goal	• Listen • Keep purpose in mind • Stay focused on objective • Use own energy and enthusiasm to help process along

4

From Controlling to Facilitating

When people are promoted to positions of leadership, or when they decide to take on a leadership role, many erroneously assume that "leadership" means to "take control," to take a directive approach with those they are leading. Taking control connotes, for many people, a directive, managerial style of leadership in which the leader decides what the followers will do, tells them what to do, and then evaluates how well they do it. However, when leaders tell others what to, they miss out on their followers' potentially valuable suggestions and opinions. They discourage questions, creativity, and risk taking. Effective team leaders rely on others' input and decision making abilities as well as their own. In today's work environments, leaders must work steadily and cooperatively with their teams as a team member as well as a team leader.

Sometimes a leader must be directive in approach. To do otherwise might cause people harm or damage an organization's reputation. At other times a leader must avoid being directive and become a facilitator, working with others to develop joint solutions.

Realistically, team leaders must wear two hats: one of team member and one of facilitator. When facilitating, it is best for a team leader to remain neutral and let the team work up a solution. However, when the team leader is a subject-matter expert and needs to be a contributing team member, he or she cannot remain neutral at all times. Team leaders must make judgments about when to remain neutral and when to make sure their opinions and ideas are expressed. In my experience, I have found that team leaders usually err in the direction of trying to influence the team too much and could do well to remain neutral more of the time. From time to time, when team progress requires it, the team leader should certainly add his or her ideas for consideration. Once these ideas have been put forth, the team leader can step back into the role of facilitator. A facilitative team leader must be careful not to dominate the team's decisions, but to simply add his or her input for consideration along with others' ideas.

> "Indeed, this is the essence of the team leader's job—
> striking the right balance between providing guidance and
> giving up control, between making tough decisions and
> letting others make them, and between doing difficult
> things alone and letting others learn how to do them"
> [Katzenbach and Smith, 1993].

Power and the Role of Leadership

Good leaders are able to operate effectively up and down a continuum from directive to facilitative. They learn how to motivate the team by allowing maximum involvement of all members whenever possible in the decision-making process. However, they know when something is truly nonnegotiable and when the team will have to be sold on an idea or decision. The strong leader knows when to tell and when to listen.

The successful team leader focuses on creating a workplace that encourages everyone to take responsibility for the success of the company. The team leader becomes a partner with team members, and team members play a partnership role with their leaders. There is less of a "we-they" approach to leading and more of a synergy between leaders and team members. To a leader-facilitator, the group is a synergistic body of diverse and valuable knowledge and experience.

The complex and dynamic nature of business today has made it necessary to spread power out over the organization, more so than in the past. Change happens so quickly and information increases and fluctuates so much that leaders must often rely on those they lead for current information as well as for its interpretation. Because information is a form of power in an organization, leaders cannot hold all the power. Today, leadership power comes largely from being able to tap the knowledge and abilities of others.

From Overresponsibility to Shared Responsibility

For teams to be productive, leaders must draw people out, listen, and incorporate their ideas. The idea that the leader is the only decision maker is a mind-set that has had to change in recent years. More progressive leaders think of themselves as "facilitators" or "catalysts"—servants or helpers of the group. Bradford and Cohen (1984), in their book *Managing for Excellence*, describe how an "overresponsible leader" can diminish the effectiveness of his or her team members (see Figure 4.1, Consequences of the Controlling Leadership Style). An overcontrolling leader gets less and less from team members because they have not participated enough in all levels of decision making. As a result, they become less and less committed to the results. In turn, the overresponsible leader takes on too much ownership for what is done. In the end, group members are not fully committed to what is planned or decided.

FIGURE 4.1. Consequences of the Controlling Leadership Style.

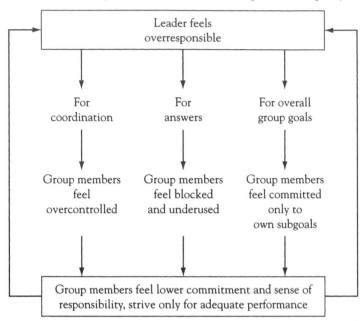

Adapted from *Managing for Excellence: The Guide to Developing High Performance in Contemporary Organizations* (p. 57) by D. L. Bradford and A. R. Cohen, copyright © 1984 by John Wiley & Sons, Inc., New York. Adapted by permission of John Wiley & Sons.

To overcome this tendency to be overly responsible, to avoid leading as if holding a horse by the reins, leaders must *place a higher value on the knowledge and experience of all group members*. Effective leaders come to be perceived almost as another group member, while making all group members feel as free to make contributions.

A Continuum of Leadership Style

The range of leadership styles can be shown on a continuum. At one end of the continuum is the autocratic, controlling leader; at the other end is the facilitative leader. A leader's position along this continuum depends on how much he or she shares the responsibility for decision making with subordinates.

The functions and behaviors of the controlling leader differ greatly from those of the facilitative leader (see Figure 4.2, Controlling Versus Facilitating Styles of Leadership). On the controlling side of the continuum, the leader retains full responsibility for the work and decisions of the team. On the facilitating side of the continuum, the leader shares that responsibility with team members. The controlling leader tells, sells, directs, decides, delegates, solves problems, and rewards people. He or she tries to control the work and the output of the team. The facilitative leader listens, empowers, supports, coaches, teaches, collaborates, and guides the team to consensus.

FIGURE 4.2. Controlling Versus Facilitating Styles of Leadership.

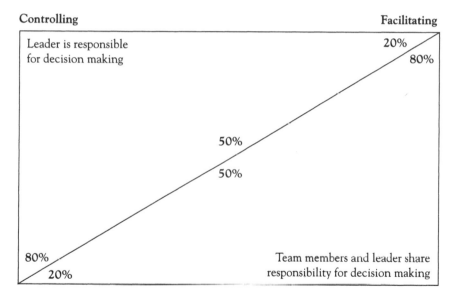

Controlling   Facilitating

Leader is responsible
for decision making   20%
                                                                        80%

                                            50%
                                        50%

80%   Team members and leader share
    20%   responsibility for decision making

Controlling leader's role	Facilitating leader's role
• Tell	• Listen
• Sell	• Ask questions
• Direct	• Direct group process
• Decide	• Coach
• Delegate	• Teach
• Solve problems	• Build consensus
• Set goals	• Share in goal setting
• Use authority to get things done	• Share in decision making
	• Empower others to get things done

A controlling, coercive style of leadership has several harmful effects. For instance, subordinates of authoritarian leaders are reluctant to reveal problems because they fear the unpleasant consequences that may result. Authoritarian approaches reduce the frequency of upward communication and affect the accuracy of communication from employees to their bosses. In fact, group members selectively send the messages that they think will bring rewards and forestall punishment. "Tell the boss what he or she wants to hear" is the principle governing their behavior.

There are several possible harmful outcomes of a team leader who takes an authoritarian approach:

- Team members may try to get on the good side of their leader or become "leader's pets."

- Excessive competitiveness and rivalry among team members results in tattling, backbiting, cheating, covering up, and gossiping; these power struggles arise out of the need for individuals to avoid punishment and to look good in the leader's eyes.

- Team members cope by becoming submissive and conforming to the team leader's demands; they may become weak in initiative and creativity and, therefore, be ineffective at problem solving and risk taking.

- Those who do not submit and conform may become rebellious and defiant, thereby frustrating other team members and weakening the work of the team.

- Others may choose to withdraw from the team relationship, either physically or psychologically; they may refuse to speak up or get involved for fear of punishing consequences.

The leader who operates on the controlling end of the continuum takes power into his or her hands and produces results, many of which are based on his or her own abilities. The facilitating leader puts the power into everyone's hands, serving as a guide and a catalyst. The facilitating leader also produces results. The difference: The facilitating leader's power is shared and often expanded because of the synergy of people working together. Thus the facilitating leader, together with others, often produces better results. Instead of giving up power, the facilitating leader expands and shares power.

but doesn't too much power create internal chaos

The Facilitative Leader

The controlling leader is more likely to see power as limited. The facilitative leader is more likely to view power as dynamic and expansive, maybe even infinite. To the facilitative leader, power is not something to be fought over but something to instill in everyone to achieve a greater goal.

very anti-human anti-survival but ethical

Under facilitative leaders, group members are more motivated to support the decisions that are made, because they feel the decisions are theirs and not someone else's. Responsibility for carrying out the decision is shared too. Group members' talents, experience, and knowledge are therefore better employed. Managers and leaders have more relevant information. Management and the group develop more trust and more overall group cohesiveness.

In facilitated teams, everyone has a chance to be and feel powerful. The goal is not to gain power but to complete the work assigned to the team. The goal is not to divide power into definable pieces but to work together to produce what could not be produced by individuals working alone.

It is the leader's view of power that governs his or her leadership style. A controlling leader views power as limited, as something to be possessed by an elite few. The facilitating leader views power as expansive, a positive force to be shared for the increased good of the organization.

Decision Making

A directive leader has generally already made up his or her mind and selects one of two approaches: (1) tell and sell others on how something will be done (the most autocratic approach) or (2) ask for opinions and support of others, acknowledge others' reactions, and then proceed as planned (a directive, but not as autocratic, approach). In today's work environment, a directive team leader runs the risk of little or no commitment from team members and may alienate those from whom he or she needs support. Motivating others with this style or approach becomes difficult, as the directive team leader must continually tell and sell team members on his or her way. If and when a directive approach must be taken, a good way to lessen the blow is to ask others to voice their reactions, acknowledge those reactions, and try to proceed in a manner that will at least accommodate people's needs where possible. Often, even though a decision has been made, there is leeway as to how that decision will be carried out. A leader who must implement a decision that team members have little or no input on may be able to involve team members in *how* that decision will be carried out.

Moving toward a more facilitative approach, a team leader operates both as a leader and as a member of the team. The leader works *with* the team to come up with a joint, mutually agreeable, solution. This approach works well when the team leader has valuable inputs to make on the content of the decision, but still needs to act as the team's facilitator. When a team leader facilitates the team in this manner, the team members and team leader collaborate to form a solution. However, when collaborating with the team, the leader must be careful not to use power to weight his or her ideas. Reverting to the use of position power moves the team leader back toward the mode of directing.

At times, a team leader may choose to take a completely neutral role with the team and not contribute his or her own ideas or opinions. When the team leader takes an entirely neutral stand, he or she directs *only* the process of what goes on and facilitates the group to come up with its best solution. The leader may pose the vision, problem, or goal and let the group decide how to proceed. Or the leader may let the group define the vision, problem, or goal. When the team leader facilitates in this way, there is generally strong support of the decision, and little or no alienation occurs between the group and the leader. When the leader remains neutral, the team members have freedom to wrestle with ideas and decide how to proceed. They may or may not want the ideas and opinions of the leader. Whether they do or not, it is the team's decision—*facilitated* by the leader but not *influenced* by the leader—that holds.

Leaders and Power

Some people may imagine that when a team leader plays a neutral role, he or she runs the risk of abdicating authority, and even responsibility as the team leader. In reality, the authority, skill, and power lie in the leader's ability to draw out the expertise and creativity of team members and, by so doing, come up with a good decision. The leader, in this case, is using *facilitative power* to motivate the team and stimulate creativity and synergy. Power is shared among the entire team and the leader, because together they have each taken roles to work toward a solution. This is a difficult place for many leaders to put themselves because, in this place, they totally rely on the combined wisdom of the team members. In fact, they enable team members to take leadership. Once team leaders overcome the fear of such a "loss of control," they find they have actually increased their power. They have empowered others to decide, act, and proceed. They have harnessed more power than they would have had being directive. And they do not have to keep pushing as hard to keep control, because they have motivated and enabled others to take charge and move forward.

When the team leader facilitates, success belongs to the team. When using this approach, an effective leader helps others achieve success and shares that success with them.

In the directive role, the leader takes control of the *content* of the team's decisions. In the facilitative role, the leader takes control of the *process*, letting the team come up with the content. This taking control of the process is not done in an autocratic way, but in a trust-building way, with concern and consideration for team members, using good facilitation skills and effective facilitation processes. The team leader can invite team members to suggest processes to use as well. In fact, team members who are accustomed to being facilitated will naturally suggest processes to use.

What Is a Facilitative Leader?

A facilitative leader is someone who acts on the premise that *a leader does not do for others what they can do for themselves*. A facilitative leader is someone who

- Listens actively
- Asks questions and listens to the whole answer
- Reserves judgment and keeps an open mind
- Actively seeks ideas and opinions from others
- Solicits different viewpoints

- Teaches others how to solve problems, without solving the problems for them
- Teaches and coaches others, without telling them what to do
- Organizes information and data so others can understand and act on it
- Models the behavior he or she would like to see in others
- Knows how to bring the right people together for a task
- Is aware of his or her own limitations and knows who is better qualified to make a decision or complete a task
- Helps people reach consensus and strives for win-win agreements
- Does not take personal credit for what other individuals or the team does, but ensures that credit goes where credit is due
- Understands that diversity can affect teamwork in positive ways
- Understands that different people are motivated by different things and is willing to work hard to address these individual needs
- Shares power and authority with others
- Encourages team members to take responsibility for issues, problems, actions, and projects
- Looks for ways to help the team achieve its goals
- Finds opportunities to reward appropriate behavior; minimizes punishment for inappropriate behavior
- Is firm about goals and flexible about the process used to reach those goals

- Has belonged to and had positive work experience with heterogeneous groups (has not been solely with people who are like himself or herself)

- Is not afraid to address conflict

- Understands and acknowledges that people's individual needs (social, personal, career, lifestyle, work preference, and so on) affect teamwork and works with, not against, these needs

Balancing Managing with Facilitating

Facilitative managers build teams that share the leadership and management responsibilities. Management duties still exist; the way they are carried out is what changes.

For example, in a facilitative organization some decisions will still be left to one person, perhaps the manager or team leader. The facilitative manager or team leader, however, consults with others before making such decisions. The information available for making decisions is richer, and therefore the decisions are usually better.

A facilitative manager may consult more with his or her team members, allowing those team members to provide information and interpretations, while still reserving the right to make the final decision. By using the group's resources, the deciding manager enriches the decision-making process and engenders group support when a decision is made that takes group members' inputs into account.

A facilitative manager may also work with his or her group to come up with a consensus decision. A consensus decision is one that is reached when all *members* of the group work together to build a solution and to support the group's decision 100 percent.

By deciding which decisions are to be made through consultation and which by consensus, the facilitative manager exercises managerial responsibility. Indeed, a difficult part of managing in a facilitative style is determining what type of decision process a situation calls for. The manager still remains accountable for the final decision, even though he or she may not have made the decision.

Empowering others to take part in decisions does not mean that employees will automatically make quality decisions. People must want to take part; in other words, they need to be *motivated* to do so. They must feel there is something in it for them. Even though they may be motivated to participate, employees may not always have the *ability* to make a decision.

Managers can help employees gain the knowledge and skills necessary to participate in decision making. And even when the ability and motivation are present, employees may still not be able to participate unless they are given the *permission, support, and resources* to do so—in other words, the authority to participate in a productive way. For example, teams may be formed and given the training and motivation to increase the number of decisions they make. However, their decision-making power is in reality nonexistent if they are limited in the amount of time they can meet or are told they cannot have any money to make changes or are not given an audience with supervisors. If they are given a job to do without the authority to do it, motivation dies and knowledge and skills are not put to use for the good of the organization.

Facilitative managers do not give up their role; on the contrary, they have important responsibilities. They have to see that things are in place for participation to be productive. They have to make sure that participation is worthwhile and will make a difference to the people who report to them (the motivation), that people's knowledge and skills are assessed and upgraded (the ability), and that people have sufficient resources and authority to participate (the permission).

Determining Your Leadership Style

The questionnaire in Exhibit 4.1 will help you reflect on your current leadership style and compare it to the leadership continuum discussed earlier in this chapter. Do you tend to be controlling or facilitating when leading others? Are you somewhere in the middle? Most of us have a natural or learned tendency toward one end of the continuum or the other. Anyone, however, can learn to adapt his or her style to be more effective.

The questionnaire will help you determine where your leadership comfort zone is and what approach you use most frequently. The final questions and the explanation following the questionnaire will guide you in determining what changes you might make in your leadership style.

Moving from a controlling to a facilitating style means change: changes in mind-set and leadership style, changes in the way leaders relate to their followers and followers relate to leaders, changes in the way work gets done, changes in the types of behavior and performance that are rewarded, and changes in the way team members relate to one another. There is no easy way to tackle all of these changes at once, nor will the transition be a smooth one.

Leaders who are making the transition to a more facilitative approach will do well to remember three principles of change:

1. Change takes *time*.
2. Change is a *process*, not a decision.
3. Change requires plenty of *experience and practice* in the new way of doing things.

EXHIBIT 4.1. Leadership Style Questionnaire.

Respond to the statements below as honestly as possible. Consider how you act in *most situations* as a team leader. Circle the *letter* of the response that best describes your behavior.

1. When discussing a difficult issue with people on my team, I most often
   a. Express my opinions and offer a solution
   b. Listen first to the opinions of others and suggest a mutual solution
   c. Ask for people's opinions and summarize what I heard

2. If team members are not attending team meetings, I
   a. Call everyone together (with suitable reward and motivation for attending) and ask team members what needs to happen to get better attendance at team meetings
   b. Go to each team member and ask each one what will improve team meeting attendance, then decide what to do
   c. Send a notice to all team members stating that meeting attendance is mandatory

3. At a meeting of my team, I am most comfortable when
   a. Listening, asking questions, and recording group inputs
   b. Presenting and/or having others present
   c. Letting someone else facilitate while I participate as a team member

4. To make sure my team is pursuing the right goals, I am most apt to
   a. Collaborate with the team to determine what the team's goals should be
   b. Review upper management's expectations with the team and then have the team define its specific goals
   c. Tell the team what its goals are, based on input I get from upper management

5. When leading a team meeting, I always
   a. Have someone take meeting notes to be distributed after the meeting
   b. Use flip charts or white boards to record team member inputs and decisions
   c. Wait until the end of the meeting and write down only the decisions and action items

6. When I take on the role of neutral facilitator, I
   a. Enjoy remaining neutral while others come up with ideas
   b. Want very badly to chime in with my opinions and solutions
   c. Am comfortable occasionally giving input to the discussion and then quickly returning to the role of neutral facilitator

EXHIBIT 4.1. Leadership Style Questionnaire, *continued*

7. When participating in a group meeting, I am
   a. Strong and outspoken in my opinions
   b. Skilled at getting both my own and others' opinions considered
   c. Skilled at drawing out the ideas of others to open new doors for creativity and problem solving

8. When leading a group meeting, I
   a. Don't know how to summarize a group discussion
   b. Am comfortable summarizing what the group has said
   c. Summarize group inputs to work to my advantage

9. When the synergy of my team leads it to a conclusion I do not support, I
   a. Tell the group I cannot support the decision
   b. Ask the group to rethink its conclusion based on evidence I cite
   c. Support the group's decision even when I don't agree 100 percent

10. When leading a team meeting, if the energy level and urgency move in a direction other than the agenda, I
    a. Invite the group to suggest alterations
    b. Alter the agenda to fit the needs of the group
    c. Stick to the agenda

11. When leading a team, I am most apt to
    a. Present some guidelines for appropriate team behavior and ask team members to add some of their own
    b. Facilitate the team to set its own guidelines for appropriate team behavior
    c. Set and publish guidelines for appropriate team behavior

12. When I am the expert on a subject the team is dealing with, I
    a. Wear two hats while facilitating the meeting: remaining neutral when possible and contributing when needed
    b. Let someone else facilitate the meeting while I act as a team member
    c. Influence the team with my advice and approach, while leading the team meeting

Scoring the Leadership Style Questionnaire

Give yourself a point score by tallying up the points related to each of your responses. Use the points designated below.

Question 1:   a = 1   Your points for Question 1:   2
                   b = 2   b
                   c = 3

Question 2:   a = 3   Your points for Question 2:   1
                   b = 2   c
                   c = 1

Question 3:   a = 3   Your points for Question 3:   1
                   b = 1   b
                   c = 2

Question 4:   a = 2   Your points for Question 4:   1
                   b = 3   c
                   c = 1

Question 5:   a = 1   Your points for Question 5:   1
                   b = 3   a
                   c = 2

Question 6:   a = 3   Your points for Question 6:   1
                   b = 1   b
                   c = 2

Question 7:   a = 1   Your points for Question 7:   2
                   b = 2   b
                   c = 3

Question 8:   a = 2   Your points for Question 8:   1
                   b = 3   c
                   c = 1

Question 9:   a = 1   Your points for Question 9:   1
                   b = 2   a
                   c = 3

Question 10:   a = 3   Your points for Question 10:   1
                   b = 2   c
                   c = 1

Question 11:   a = 2   Your points for Question 11:   3
                   b = 3   b
                   c = 1

Question 12:   a = 2   Your points for Question 12:   1
                   b = 3   c
                   c = 1

                               Point Total: 16

EXHIBIT 4.1. Leadership Style Questionnaire, *continued*

Interpreting Your Score

If you scored in the *low range*, from 12 to 18 points, you lean toward being a controlling team leader. You can undoubtedly benefit by becoming more collaborative and facilitative in your approach to team leadership. There are many times when it will benefit you and your organization to actively solicit and incorporate the ideas of others in your decisions. There are times when the best approach will be to guide others to come up with the best solution. Gaining skill and practice in facilitation will broaden and enhance your leadership skills, giving you more opportunities to be an effective leader. This book will help you move along that path.

If you scored in the *medium range*, from 19 to 30 points, you are definitely a collaborative team leader and somewhat comfortable with facilitating. You tend to work with others by contributing your ideas as well as encouraging others to contribute theirs. You work toward agreement by trying to incorporate both yours and others' ideas. There are times when a good leader should remain neutral and facilitate others' coming up with a solution. Improving your fundamental facilitation skills and getting more practice as a facilitator will help you expand and refine your facilitative leadership skills.

If you scored in the *high range*, from 31 to 36 points, you are a highly facilitative leader and quite comfortable with facilitating. This is your preferred way to lead. You are effective at drawing others out and getting them to come to a decision. You are likely to be a sought-after team leader. Remember, however, that the facilitating approach, though powerful and effective, should not be used to the exclusion of other methods. There may be times when your team will need you to be more directive or involved in the content of a decision. Also, look carefully at the L.E.A.D. model (Figure 3.2) and understand that the leader's tasks are not all facilitative.

No matter how you scored, remember there are times when facilitation is by far the best approach and times when another approach is called for.

Now respond to this statement: In my organization, there are

a. Taboos against being facilitative; only aggressive and outspoken leaders are rewarded
b. Sufficient role models for being a facilitative leader
c. Expectations that leaders will be facilitative, but with time pressure that makes this difficult

If you answered "a," be aware that it will be hard for you to become a facilitative leader in your current work environment. Not impossible, but hard. Try your facilitation skills out in the community, in your family, or with colleagues who are more facilitative by nature.

If you answered "b," you are fortunate. Your road to becoming a facilitative leader is a much easier one. Use these role models as teachers and mentors.

If you answered "c," you are not alone. Today it is common for organization cultures to espouse teamwork and facilitation without backing it up with resources and active support. Many, however, are trying and some are doing a wonderful job of it. You can be part of helping your organization make important gains through teamwork and facilitation.

Leaders seeking change must acknowledge the vast effort it takes and must not give up when it takes more time and practice than anticipated. Change is not on a switch, like a light that goes on and off, but is a process—sometimes a very long one. Leaders who effectively implement change make sure that their teams have plenty of opportunities to practice new ways of doing things while they go about their day-to-day activities.

Here are some additional principles that will help leaders make the transition to facilitation:

- Make one or two changes at a time. Do not tackle everything at once.

- Allow time for change to take place. Change is never easy, and people need time to learn new ways of working together.

- Reward people's efforts to change; otherwise, they will not change.

- Keep the goal in mind. The goal is not to have a team but to increase productivity and employee satisfaction.

- Accomplish something daily toward the goal. Do not let time go by without moving in the desired direction.

- Use planning and regular evaluation of progress as tools to move toward the goal.

- Have patience with people. Change is difficult and even threatening for some.

- Do not play God. Be realistic but positive about what you can accomplish given your company's culture and the constraints placed on you. Acknowledge that you cannot change the organization alone, and plan accordingly.

Perhaps you want to make some changes in your leadership style but still have a nagging question: "Where do I start?" You may feel overwhelmed by the number of things you want to change or you may not understand how to apply the ideas presented here to your own situation.

Here is a suggested process for making the transition from a controlling style of leadership to a more facilitative one. First, while reading this book, list the things you would like to change in the way your team or group works together or in how you lead the group. Think in terms of making these improvements over many months to several years. Second, ask yourself what strengths, support systems, and other resources you already have that can help you make these improvements. Plan to use these strengths to your advantage when you begin to make changes. Third, break these big changes down into small steps. If you want to start listening more to people, for example, write down the actions you can take to accomplish this goal. For example:

- Ask at least three questions of other people each day. Then make an effort to listen without interrupting.

- Take a course in listening.

- Ask a friend to tell you when you interrupt and when you appear to demonstrate good listening skills.

What to Expect

People may resist change, even when it is for the better. Change disrupts people's lives, challenges their beliefs about themselves and their world, and creates confusion and disorientation. Therefore, do not expect others to welcome the "new you" or to be supportive, even when you believe you are acting this way for their benefit. In fact, you may find subordinates and followers almost antagonistic at first, even when you begin to listen more and ask for their input.

Why does this happen? When you begin to draw people out and listen to them, they may distrust you at first. They will be wary, watching for your reactions. They may simply avoid saying anything, afraid that what they say may be used against them. Unless you have been a good listener in the past, they may not be used to expressing their feelings and ideas to you.

Another typical reaction is that people will, when finally asked how they feel and think, vent many of their frustrations all at once. They will take the opportunity to talk about everything they do not like. This deluge of negativity may be difficult to deal with. But the way to handle it is to listen and take notes. Ask people for clarification or examples when they are vague, so you can more fully understand the extent of their complaints. Demonstrate your ability to listen without sermonizing and without judgment or bias. Try not to become defensive. Avoid making promises. You may explain that you are listening so that you can begin to see ways to involve them more in planning and decision making and that you will be trying to help them solve some of these problems in the future.

Summary

Facilitating is a legitimate, useful, and often essential approach when leading others. Good leaders understand that their actions will take them up and down the leadership continuum from controlling to facilitating. They are also aware that, in today's work environment, moving toward the facilitating end of this continuum is often the only way to achieve the level of teamwork needed to reach goals.

5

Facilitation Ignites Team Spirit

Team leadership and facilitation go hand in hand. Without facilitation, teams consistently fail, and with competent facilitation, a team has a much greater chance of succeeding. Team leaders must know how to draw out, structure, and lead participation and communication in their group, because the entire team must define, plan, and assign the work. This type of leadership requires facilitation skills, critical when group members must work closely together.

Facilitation Defined

Facilitation is the process of making a group's work easier by structuring and guiding the participation of group members so that everyone is involved and contributes. In this sense, facilitation is a leadership skill that is highly important to any kind of teamwork. Facilitation is used during group meetings, one-on-one, and in any setting in which communication is needed to further the work of a team (or collaborative partnership).

Facilitators do not control or dominate. They provide opportunities for team members to collaborate, solve problems, make decisions, define processes they will use, and learn better how to work with one another and within the organization. The skilled facilitator helps the team find its best information, cull its creativity, and marshal its efforts. This is not done through telling and selling, but rather through asking, listening, structuring communication, and summarizing. With a skilled leader-facilitator, the team can realize the synergy that comes when a group of people pools its knowledge and works toward a defined goal.

The Value of Facilitation

Imagine a team with everyone speaking his or her mind, with each team member set on a decision (but on different decisions), with a leader who is an expert on the topic at hand (also with an idea about what the decision should be), and no one structuring the discussion so the team can come to agreement. This is a typical team without someone facilitating. This is a typical team in an environment in which those with the most power push their decisions through. This is a typical team that may or may not realize its need for a neutral facilitator. In a team such as this, the person(s) with the strongest influence—or the most dominant person(s)—controls the entire team, and the team as a whole loses momentum and motivation.

Unfortunately, many teams find themselves in this predicament. They do not have someone to lead them in such a way that their best work can be done. The team leader is more interested in the content of the team's decisions than in the fact that someone must facilitate collaboration. What many teams need, and what teamwork needs in general, is someone who will use facilitation skills to assure that the kind of communication that will move groups forward will happen.

The level of work expected of people makes facilitation skills important to team leaders and superworkers alike. To understand another's motivation, barriers, prejudices, needs, and knowledge helps people strategize the approach to take. Listening well gives people the greatest power and tool of all—information. Asking astute questions gives people the best information for the task at hand. Workers have to be skilled at gathering, summarizing, and organizing information and drawing conclusions from it.

In busy organizations today, everyone is overworked and stretched. Jobs are defined broadly, and people are expected to determine how and where their job fits in with the work of others. To do this, employees cannot work in isolation from one another. They must find out what others do, what the company as a whole does, and how their jobs affect those of others. People must come together to solve complex problems involving several jobs or departments. Each person must learn to draw out others and facilitate conversations and meetings to accomplish the work. Facilitation skills fuel collaboration and cooperation with others.

Over the years, I have witnessed the progress of many teams and projects. Repeatedly, the teams or projects that have not had a facilitator or a leader with strong facilitation skills have struggled greatly—and many have failed. When a team is stranded without anyone to facilitate meetings and to act as a facilitative leader, it is hamstrung from the beginning. Teamwork, in general, goes better when someone facilitates open, focused, and structured communication throughout the project or life of the team.

Values-Based Facilitation

Leaders cannot afford to work only on the level of facilitation *skills*. They must also work at the deeper level of facilitation *values*. One can perform and operate at a skill level, and this will render benefits. However, *attitudes, values,* and *beliefs* are at the core of facilitation. Without supporting values, the process of facilitation will be shallow and insincere.

People can be taught and required to act a certain way in the work environment. These actions may not be natural or intuitive, but they can be performed to a certain level of skill, even if the person doesn't really believe in the value of the actions. This type of behavior will usually be minimally effective. In the case of time or other pressure, the person may resort to the more "natural" behavior. If, however, a person's behavior is in alignment with his or her core values and beliefs, the behavior will be consistent and genuine, even under pressure.

Figure 5.1 illustrates how values are at the core of our beliefs, attitudes, and behaviors. What we value and place high importance on, what we really care about, influences what we believe. What we believe forms our attitudes, and our attitudes lead to our behavior.

FIGURE 5.1. How Values Drive Behavior Model.

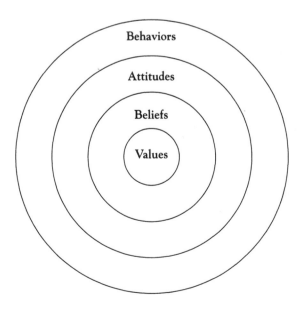

When a leader values people and their diversity of ideas and abilities, that leader is more likely to instinctively use facilitation skills to draw out the opinions and viewpoints of the people he or she leads. If a leader values the ideas and abilities of other people, that same leader is apt to believe that people have valuable ideas. What follows is an attitude of awareness of and openness to others. Certain behaviors will then follow this attitude: a willingness to seek others out, to ask questions, to listen, to reflect back what has been said, and to collaborate with others when necessary, rather than consistently operate alone. Good facilitation skills (behaviors) in this case are habitual and instinctual, not "learned" and painstakingly applied. Sometimes, however, when people learn and practice facilitation skills, they become more aware, sensitive, and respectful of the viewpoints of others. In some cases, we grow new values by applying new skills. The skills themselves open up our minds to value something new.

The ability to lead in today's fluid, project-oriented, multi-team, global environment requires more than skill. It requires emotional maturity, a high tolerance for diversity, an adaptability to change, an affinity for two-way communication, and heart. From heart comes the true desire to care for people, to treat them as equals, as partners, to both empathize with and challenge them to do their best. The only real good listening comes from the heart. A good leader must listen. How else can he or she strategize the work, participate collaboratively in a team, take others sufficiently into consideration to both support them and receive their support?

The leader is a facilitator of process, the umbrella personality under which dynamics occur that lead to group output. Skills tell one how to act when and what to do if certain things occur. A deeper level of understanding, along with a belief set that values participation, will intuitively guide the leader to infuse teamwork into all aspects of work and relationships. For example, a facilitative leader will intuitively ask questions of those with both more and less "position power" than he or she has. *Level* is not the issue. *Behavior* is the issue. And behavior is based on beliefs and values. If a leader believes that all people have something to contribute, his or her behavior will support this belief. If a leader believes that collaboration will produce higher quality or more appropriate output, the behavior will follow.

Facilitative Behavior and Skills

Good facilitators are respectful of other people's time. They are selective with questions, e-mails, requests, meetings, and involvement in what others are doing. They are aware that, by facilitating their relationships, they are building a trust-level relationship for the future. Good facilitators are efficient with how they use other people's time, energy, information, creativity, and loyalty. The good facilitator knows he or she never works in isolation. For any given piece of work, there are always the questions: "Who is my 'team' in this process?" "Whom do I need for information, ideas, talent?" "Who has special knowledge and experience that will enhance this work?" "From whom will I need buy-in, ongoing help, feedback, resources, and communication?"

Certain behaviors and communication skills are necessary to facilitate teamwork. These include asking focused and open-ended questions, listening, summarizing, recording, asking for agreement, getting back to people, and passing on information.

Several things need to be present for a successful facilitation to occur, whether in a one-on-one discussion or in a team meeting:

- Focused goal or objective
- Open communication

- Key points recorded
- Key points summarized
- Mutual agreement reached, or decision postponed
- Decisions made as to who will do what by when

Using a facilitation process may take more time initially, but in the end there is less resistance to moving forward when people have collaborated in the decision and determined how to proceed. It has been proven again and again that people support what they help create. Facilitative leaders are aware of the need to draw fully on the vast knowledge and experience of their employees, to gain employees' help, support, and commitment up front. They have seen how top-down methods become bogged down in misinterpretation, poor communication, and poor decision making. More is required of individual employees, but letting people work too much alone, without communication and collaboration, causes redundant, wasted, and inappropriate efforts.

Facilitation Myths

Like anything that is not fully understood, the concept of facilitation conjures up, for some people, images of support groups, "touchy-feely" team-building sessions, and the venting of frustrations. Some of the common myths about facilitation follow, along with the realities of how it works.

- *Facilitation is a loose approach to management that invites disorder and chaos.* On the contrary, a well-facilitated team has clear boundaries and ground rules. Within those boundaries, however, there is room for creativity and flexibility. Facilitating leaders spend time planning how they will work with their people, how meetings will be run, and how issues will be communicated and dealt with. When they invite participation, they do so within a structure that will ensure productivity. In fact, good facilitators place a high value on both structure and creativity.

• *A facilitative leader simply agrees to everything the team wants; truly strong and powerful leaders would not want to appear weak in front of their people and would therefore not ask for help and support.* On the contrary, to be a facilitative leader takes strength of character and a strong sense of oneself. It takes courage and wisdom to allow others to make decisions and to support those decisions. It takes a strong person to set clear boundaries without destroying team morale. It takes wisdom to determine correctly which decisions can better be made by the team and which must be reserved for management. It takes a strong person to seek advice and input from others and still make the best decision.

• *Facilitative leaders give up their power and control.* Actually, they have access to more power, because they empower others to act; they receive power from the people they lead. Facilitative leadership increases the power of a team as a whole and the sphere of influence for that team. Facilitators do not give up control; rather, they control things (such as meetings) in a way that allows others to produce their highest quality work.

• *It won't work in this culture!* Many corporate cultures are not very receptive to participation and involvement on the part of their people. Yet determined leaders can gradually and quietly introduce participation and involvement. In one-on-one meetings, the leader-facilitator can demonstrate a willingness to listen and to explore the merits of an idea before judging it. Decisions reached in group meetings can be designated "team decisions."

- *Facilitation takes too much time. We won't get anything done.* Some people fear that the team approach requires too many meetings in which too much time is spent hearing everyone out and arguing every point. Facilitation does encourage individual expression, discussion, and even disagreement. Within a planned meeting structure, however, participation can be and should be highly productive. Building consensus takes more time initially, but in the long run, consensus means more support and commitment from those who must make something happen.

- *Facilitation encourages anarchy.* Again, with guidance and structure provided by the facilitator, people can focus on the issue and deal within the realm of their authority. On the other hand, for facilitation to work, some decisions still must filter down from management to workers. This is not anarchy; this is involved decision making.

- *The democracy of facilitation will water down the quality of decisions.* On the contrary, an effective decision-by-consensus process ensures that decisions are well thought out, realistic, and motivating to employees. Support occurs naturally when key players are involved in making the decision.

- *Once we start a facilitative approach, we will have to do everything this way.* On the contrary, some decisions can be reserved for certain levels or roles. In fact, facilitative leaders can take a strong stand about the situations that call for participation and those that do not. However, most companies have erred in the other direction: not allowing enough decisions to be made by employees. When a facilitative approach works well, people can be expected to want to use it frequently. Leaders will have to determine when facilitation is appropriate.

Summary

Good teamwork calls for a balance between structure and freedom and process and content. Whether in ad hoc, one-on-one, or planned team meetings, good facilitation ensures this importance balance.

6

The New Team Leader

If teamwork is vital to organizations today, then equally vital is the team leader, the person who structures, inspires, and facilitates teamwork. Cultures oriented to teamwork require team leaders at all levels in the organization. Individuals, teams, and higher level managers must understand what teamwork is, what a good work team is, and how to participate in teamwork. Leading a work team requires exercising the ability to work both within the team as a working member and just outside the team as a facilitator.

Team leaders, managers, individual workers, and team members all are more productive when they have the ability to help people cooperate, communicate, and collaborate. Working solo gets people into trouble, especially when they need the support of others for a project to succeed.

Today's Team Leader

The new team leader is someone who assumes team leadership, whether formally or informally. In today's work environment, the role of a team leader is not so much a formal designation as it is a situational determination. A team leader can broadly be defined as "someone who takes action to facilitate teamwork to accomplish a goal." A more narrow definition of team leader is "someone who is formally designated as a team leader by management and/or by a team and who takes action to facilitate teamwork within that team."

Generally speaking, anyone can be a team leader informally: individual contributors, managers, team leaders, team members—all may take on a team leadership role when needed. Others take on the role of team leadership in more formal ways, such as leading project teams or managing departments. Informal team leadership is called for in one-on-one interactions, in ad hoc small group discussions, on formal "teams," and in many other situations.

Who Is a Team Leader?

It is difficult to pin down just who is a team leader in today's dynamic work environments. Managers are the team leaders of their direct reports. It is not unusual for a manager to have several teams to coordinate, some of which he or she may also be leading. Project leaders often become team leaders because they must marshal the efforts of a group of people to oversee and complete the project. Some people are designated as team leaders. From time to time, a team member may step in to fill the role of a team leader, or the role of team leader may be rotated among team members. The nature of someone's job may call for team leadership, even though it may never be referred to as such. For example, a salesperson may have to coordinate communication and activity between his or her company and vendors and customers to meet the needs of a particular customer. When a sale is complex, numerous people, a number of functions, and several organizations may be involved in a kind of team effort to negotiate and deliver on the sale. A salesperson may not succeed if he or she cannot lead such a team effort.

In more mature, high-performing teams, rotating leadership is practiced. Different members, depending on their knowledge or experience in leading a group, lead the team for a period of time. An advanced or enhanced responsibility of the team leader is to develop team members' abilities to lead.

The Role of a Team Leader

The role of a team leader is a critical one. Without the team leader, a team may communicate and collaborate poorly, members may go their separate ways, important administrative and coordinating details may fall through the cracks, and creativity and synergy may not occur at all. Someone must facilitate the team's communication and connection with itself as well as with the rest of the organization.

Depending on the nature of the team, a team leader's duties may simply be to facilitate discussions, as in one-on-one or ad hoc, small teams. This team leader may not have the formal designation of "team leader" but may accomplish his or her work through initiating and leading a team effort. The team effort may be as brief as a meeting in the hall or as long as there is a working relationship between two or more people.

In other situations, a person may be designated a "team leader" or "project manager" and be given the more formal role of team leadership. In this role, the team leader may have to motivate and coordinate others to accomplish tasks and responsibilities over time, while taking on the more complete role of group leadership. Both types of team leaders, the ad hoc, temporary leader and the formally designated "team leader," will seek the support and involvement of other people and will accomplish this (or not) through the use of their communication skills and their ability to motivate others to work together.

It is difficult to describe exactly what the role of a team leader is, as organizations must adapt the role to their individual needs. Each team leader must work with his or her organization to carve out just what that role is. However, it is helpful to examine and understand the traditional role of a team leader.

The traditional role of a team leader is fourfold: (1) to manage and coordinate the team so that it does its best work, (2) to provide resources to the team, (3) to link the team and its work to the rest of the organization, and (4) to be a contributing team member. As coordinator of the team, the team leader's responsibilities include coordinating the team's meetings, seeing that administrative details are taken care of, and overseeing the team's activities. The team leader ensures that team records are kept and that all important documentation is available to the team as needed. As resource provider, the team leader sees to it that the team has adequate meeting facilities and supplies, as well as money and support for other necessities. The team leader is the main channel between the team and the rest of the organization and, in this capacity, alerts the team to changes or problems in the system that impact the team. The team leader removes blocks and barriers to the team's success, when possible. "Ultimately it is the leader's responsibility to create and maintain channels that enable team members to do their work" (Scholtes, 1988).

A team leader may do some or all of the following:

- Initiate team meetings, notify team members, secure facility and supplies
- See that team meetings are effective
- Facilitate the team to determine appropriate goals

- Keep the team focused on what it is supposed to be doing
- Define boundaries to the team: what the team is expected/ not expected to do (or collaborate with the team members to do so)
- Keep open channels of communication between the team and the larger organization
- Act as a project manager for the work of the team (or see that someone does this)
- Procure resources for the team (facilitator, supplies, subject-matter experts, funding, and so forth)
- Clarify the organization's expectations of the team
- Integrate the work of the team with other teams
- Explain and, if necessary, defend, the process the team is using to do its work
- Troubleshoot to ensure team productivity
- Contribute to the work of the team (as a team member) without dominating or over-influencing, without "pulling rank"
- Make sure team members are clear about their individual action items and commitments
- Make sure team efforts are documented and made available as needed to the team, team sponsor, and necessary others
- Remove blocks and barriers to the team's success, when possible

The above responsibilities may also fall on the superworker who is taking initiative to get involvement, information, or commitment from others to get his or her job done. Even when two people work casually together, some of these responsibilities will fall to one or both people. When working together, it helps when everyone takes on some of the leadership, which means that there may be several people facilitating the productive interactions of a group of people.

Characteristics of a Good Team Leader

A good team leader exhibits many or all of the following characteristics:

- Knows when to act as a facilitator
- Is skilled at helping groups solve problems
- Knows how to develop, maintain, and motivate teamwork
- Is a model of what is expected
- Listens well
- Encourages others to participate in decisions, plans
- Genuinely values the knowledge, information, and expertise of every team member and knows how to draw out that knowledge
- Pitches in and does some of what team members do, when necessary
- Knows how to coach and inspire
- Knows how to help people focus
- Develops team members' level of performance without threat to self
- Empathizes with what the team struggles with
- Is willing not to be "the expert"
- Is comfortable with relying on the expertise of others
- Understands and anticipates change

- Fosters team communication both electronically and face-to-face

Challenges Team Leaders Face

Teams must operate in environments that are not always open to teamwork. In any work environment, both supportive and hindering forces co-exist. Team leaders must recognize these forces within their own organizations and work to maintain or increase the supportive forces and to lessen or eliminate the hindering ones.

Hindering forces (elements that increase the likelihood that teamwork will be ignored or undermined) may include

- Fast pace
- Pressure to make decisions quickly
- Individuals rewarded for "heroic" work, not for teamwork
- Team members burdened with too much work
- Lack of people with facilitation skills
- Leaders who do not value facilitation
- Lack of support for the effort it takes to build trust, collaboration, and teamwork
- Atmosphere where teamwork is expected but not rewarded
- Elitist style of upper management (closes others out, guards information, makes decisions without consulting others)

Below are some examples of supportive forces, elements that increase the likelihood that teamwork will flourish. Effective team leaders will focus on increasing these forces as much as possible:

- Variety of input needed in decision making
- Tasks, projects, and work that require cooperation

- Less hierarchical organization (or the formal hierarchy operates in team-like fashion)
- An organization that is accustomed to working in teams
- Leaders who model teamwork, not simply espouse it
- People who prefer teamwork and are comfortable with it
- Buy-in required for implementation
- Information readily available for people to do their work
- Technical and social avenues that encourage quick and frequent communication
- Nonpunishing atmosphere when people make mistakes
- People willing to give and receive constructive feedback
- People motivated by work and collaboration, versus people motivated by self-advancement

What supporting and hindering forces are present in your own organization? What can your team do to lessen the hindering forces and strengthen the supporting forces? Where might you make a difference as a leader? As a team leader? As a team member? As an individual contributor or superworker?

Summary

Today's new team leader is anyone who must initiate and lead teamwork to get work done. Because teams are an important and often preferred way of getting things done in organizations, much responsibility has come to rest on the shoulders of designated team leaders. A team leader is generally thought of as the coordinating focus of the team, the one who directs and facilitates team members to come together to do their best work. The exact role of team leader must be defined in each organization (and perhaps within each team) and tailored to that organization's needs and structure.

personalized leadership

PART THREE

Facilitating Productive Team Communication

One of the keys to getting people to work well together is open communication. Each step of the L.E.A.D. model requires active communication:

- *Lead with a clear purpose.* The leader and team must articulate the team's goals and purpose. This requires open and thoughtful discussion, the freedom to disagree, brainstorming, and active listening.

- *Empower to participate.* Open communication must be allowed and encouraged if people are to participate in ways that will enhance teamwork and achieve results.

- *Aim for consensus.* Reaching consensus requires time for questioning, listening, clarifying, augmenting, summarizing, and documenting.

- *Direct the process.* Much of the "process" that the leader directs is that of communication, both inside and outside the team.

Chapter Seven lays out a simple process for facilitating one-on-one discussions. This approach brings people to productive, mutual agreement and helps team leaders empower others to take responsibility. Chapter Eight discusses the merits and disadvantages of various communication tools and offers advice to team leaders on how to use electronic and face-to-face communication in teams that are scattered geographically.

7

Facilitating One on One

Anyone who takes a leadership role in organizations will benefit from the ability to conduct effective one-on-one meetings with others. Meetings between the leader and one other team member serve several key purposes. They keep the leader in touch with what is going on with each person on the team. They provide the leader an opportunity to give positive feedback, to confront problems early, and to work collaboratively with individuals. One of the most important purposes is to give the leader a chance to show interest and concern for each person. Important work also is done in one-on-one meetings, such as setting goals, solving problems, making decisions, bringing problems or concerns to the surface, providing support, giving feedback on progress, and building consensus.

Purpose of One-on-One Meetings

One-on-one meetings are for issues that concern the leader and one other individual. Whenever possible, these issues should be addressed as they arise. Then, when the team members are together, they will not have unsolved individual problems to deal with.

This chapter deals with three facilitator techniques that are particularly useful in one-on-one meetings:

- Consensus building
- Problem solving
- Constructive confrontation

For clarity, these techniques are presented separately. In real life they are often used in conjunction. A good facilitator can use any one or a combination of these techniques when the situation warrants.

Building Consensus One on One

An effective team leader must know how to reach consensus, or come to a mutually acceptable agreement, with a team member. (Building consensus in a group meeting is covered in Chapter Fourteen.) Whether the task is setting a goal, making a joint decision, or planning how to proceed on a project, building consensus is important in one-on-one settings. Here are four simple steps leaders can use to facilitate the process of reaching agreement with another person:

1. Draw out the other person's ideas
2. Show understanding
3. Offer one's own ideas
4. Work toward a solution that will meet both people's needs

These four steps aim for win-win, instead of win-lose, outcomes.

To achieve the first step, drawing out the other person's ideas, the facilitative leader asks open-ended questions. These are questions that cannot be answered with a yes or no or one or two words. Open-ended questions invite the other person to share opinions, ideas, and experiences that shed light on the subject. (Chapter Eleven covers open-ended questions in more detail.)

After asking an open-ended question, the facilitative leader pauses for a response. While the other person is speaking, he or she listens actively. Listening actively is a complex skill that many people do not fully understand. To listen actively one must be alert and nonjudgmental. Here are some ways you can practice:

- Listen to every word the other person says
- Watch for nonverbal clues to the full meaning of what the other person is saying
- Avoid distractions: fidgeting, noise, phone calls, and so on
- Use eye contact, head nodding, and an attentive posture to show attention
- Avoid thinking ahead to what to say next
- Do not interrupt
- Reserve judgment, but rather put energy and attention into understanding fully what the other person is saying
- Ask questions to encourage less talkative people to continue or to obtain more information
- Be aware of biases you may have toward the speaker and work to overcome the effect these may have on your ability to really listen and understand that person (for example, you may have difficulty listening to the person because of the way he or she talks, dresses, or looks; because of past difficulties you have had working with that person or that type of person; or because of your own racial, ethnic, religious, age, or other prejudices)

The second step toward reaching consensus is to show understanding. Before presenting your own ideas or reacting to the other person's ideas, let him or her know that you understand those ideas. Briefly paraphrase what the person has said; then pause to encourage a response. This technique will test whether you have truly understood what the other person said. Once you have listened to and understood the other person, you will have earned the right to share your ideas.

In fact, offering your ideas is the third step in the consensus-building process. But be sure to build on the other person's ideas. To increase your chance of being understood, state your ideas briefly and clearly. If you feel strongly about something, say so and give reasons why you believe the way you do. Pause and allow the other person to ask questions.

The fourth step is to work toward a solution that meets both people's needs. This step usually involves working through differences. You can often overcome clear differences of opinion by summarizing the two points of view and then building a solution that will satisfy you both. For example, you might say, "So what's important to you is to finish the Biltmore project before starting the Lincoln assignment. And what I need is to make some progress on the Lincoln assignment before the end of the quarter. Let's look for a way to satisfy us both."

In summary, here are the four steps you can use to reach consensus:

1. Draw out the other person's ideas

2. Show understanding

3. Offer your ideas

4. Work toward a solution that meets both people's needs

Problem Solving One on One

One-on-one problem solving addresses two types of problems: those that the team member "owns" and must solve single-handedly and those that the leader and team member must solve jointly.

Team-Member-Owned Problems

It has already been noted that one of the key roles of a facilitative leader is to help people solve their own problems. When someone comes to you with a problem that is clearly personal—a problem with managing his or her own time or getting along with another team member, for example—it is tempting to give advice. Telling people how to solve their problems is a natural instinct. However, people usually resist changing their ways. Your suggestions are likely to be refuted or ignored. You may hear phrases such as "I wish I could, but . . ." or "That would probably work if only I didn't . . ." or "Every time I try that it doesn't work because . . . ."

A healthier and more productive technique used by psychologists is also useful for team leaders. The technique is to acknowledge the problem and get the person to see it as his or her own. Peck (1978, p. 32) emphasizes the importance of people's taking responsibility for their problems in this way: "We cannot solve life's problems except by solving them. We can only solve a problem when we say, 'This is *my* problem and it's up to me to solve it.'"

An effective leader can help others take responsibility for their problems by helping them learn problem-solving techniques—not by solving the problems for them. Leaders are often so intent on reaching goals that they cut the process short, coming up with solutions to the problems of others. What happens is a "Catch 22" situation, in which the team leader tells a team member what to do to solve a problem, the team member resists the suggestion, the problem therefore remains, and the team leader ends up having to step in and solve the problem.

A more effective approach is to acknowledge that the team member has a problem and to ask how he or she thinks the problem can be solved. For example, let us assume that Dan, one of your team members, has come to you with a problem. He is having trouble getting along with Sandy, with whom he is working on a project. Sandy has failed to meet her deadlines, putting Dan in a bind to meet his own goals. You believe this is a problem Dan can and should handle on his own. You say, "Dan, I agree with you. You do have a problem. What ideas do you have for working this thing out?" This approach accomplishes several things:

- You avoid taking on Dan's problem.
- You acknowledge Dan's problem and encourage him to act on it.
- You suggest that Dan already has some ideas about how to solve the problem.

The first step is to get Dan to agree that this is his problem and not someone else's. Until he accepts this responsibility, he is likely to resist taking action to solve the problem. Instead, he may continue to blame Sandy. Once Dan has accepted ownership of the problem, he is ready for your help in figuring out how to solve it. Remember that you are not solving the problem for him. You are simply giving him a process for solving it himself.

By using open-ended questions, you can guide another person through a step-by-step, problem-solving process. Most experts agree that about six key steps are involved in solving a problem.

Here is one version: *solving a problem:*

1. Identify the problem or goal
2. Generate alternative solutions
3. Establish objective criteria
4. Decide on a solution that best fits the criteria
5. Proceed with the solution
6. Evaluate the solution

To help another person *identify the problem*, which is the first step, ask one or more of the following questions:

- What seems to be the problem?
- How do you see the problem?
- What seems to be causing the problem?
- If the problem were solved, what would happen?

If the person is struggling to set personal or professional goals, ask

- What are you trying to achieve?
- Where do you want to end up?

During this first step, it is natural and desirable to let the person talk about his or her feelings relating to the problem. People often cannot work on solving a problem until they have a chance to vent their feelings about it.

To help the person to move on to the second step and *generate alternative solutions*, say something like "You have identified the problem (or goal) as . . . . What are some possible solutions?" Suggest that the other person think of as many ways as possible to solve the problem or achieve the goal.

Then help the person move on to the third step, *establish objective criteria,* by asking "What, if any, stipulations do you want to put on your solution? What must your solution achieve? What would you like your solution to accomplish or not accomplish?" Some possible answers are

- "I'd like the solution to decrease my hours at work, rather than increase them."

- "The solution must help me meet the deadlines on my two critical projects."

- "I don't want the quality of my work to suffer on my two critical projects."

Next, to lead the person to the fourth step, *decide on a solution that best fits the criteria,* ask, "Which of the solutions you discussed earlier will best meet these criteria?" There may be more than one. If so, ask which one best fits the criteria and is the least difficult to act on.

At this point, you have coached the other person through the first four steps of a six-step process. Notice that you have not told him or her what the solution to the problem is. You have guided the person through the four steps by asking questions and helping him or her to think through each step. Thus, you can now point out that the person has identified his or her own solution, and you can ask whether anything is impeding the fifth step, which is to *proceed with the solution.* Offer some support, if appropriate. For example, you might offer to check back with the person in a few days to see how the solution is going.

The sixth step in the process is to *evaluate the solution.* In a few days, you can ask the person, "How well did the solution work?" To the end, this process keeps you from misappropriating the problem and helps you facilitate the other person's finding a solution.

Problems Requiring Joint Resolution

The second type of problem addressed by one-to-one problem solving is the kind that you and another person must solve jointly. Both of you have enough at stake to be willing to work on a solution. Again, you can use the six-step problem-solving model. However, instead of helping the other person solve the problem, you will offer your own ideas as well. As you move through each step, build consensus.

1. Seek the other person's ideas

2. Show understanding

3. Offer your ideas

4. Work toward a solution that meets both people's needs

To start the joint problem-solving process, you can ask, "How do you see the problem?" Show the other person that you understand his or her point of view: "I see. You see the problem as. . . ." Then offer your ideas about what you think the problem is, building on the other person's ideas when you can. "I agree with what you said about. . . . I see the problem as. . . ." Build a definition of the problem from both viewpoints. Then move on to the next step, which is to generate alternative solutions. Once more, build consensus as you generate solutions: "What possible solutions do you see?" The remaining four steps in the problem-solving process unfold in similar fashion.

The consensus model is not meant to be so rigidly followed that it is counterproductive. Its main purpose is to remind you to listen first, to give others an opportunity to speak up without interruption, and to show that you understand what the other person has said. When generating alternative solutions, for example, it may be more natural for both the team leader and the team member to contribute ideas and to build on one another's ideas. The consensus model reminds more directive, controlling leaders to stop and listen, not to dominate the conversation. Following the model perfectly is not the object. The object is to build consensus by making certain that both people's ideas are taken into account.

Constructive Confrontation

From time to time, you must bring up a problem to a team member. If that problem has to do with his or her performance—a performance you would like to change—you are dealing with the need to confront. The word "confront" frequently connotes strong and negative feelings. Many people will avoid direct confrontation at all costs and will try all sorts of ways to deal with the problem indirectly. They may first avoid the problem or hint around at it. They may sneak it into the conversation so it will not be too offensive. They may become angry, be sarcastic, or find some way to get back at the other person. But none of these approaches works well.

As a facilitative leader, you can use a more constructive method for dealing with others' performance problems. First, be direct and to the point. If you have a problem, say so up front without camouflaging it. Second, be specific about what the problem is. State the facts as they relate to the specific problem. It helps to tell the other person what you expected would happen and explain what did happen from your viewpoint. Third, keep a *positive* and constructive tone and manner. Angry, accusatory behavior will alienate the other person, putting him or her on the defensive. Fourth, give the other person a *chance to respond* so you can begin to work out a solution. Ask, "What happened?" Remember to use an open, nonaccusatory tone of voice. Then pause and let the other person respond. Listen and do not interrupt. Ask questions to clarify what the other person has said.

Once you have brought the problem to the surface, you may need to explain why it is a problem. Tell the other person about the consequences of his or her behavior. Specify what you need from the other person. Determine what you will do and what the other person will do to resolve the problem. Determine the specific things that have to be done, specify when (time or date) they must be completed, and plan the next time you will get together.

Constructive confrontation avoids some of the common problems associated with confrontation. It deals with a specific here-and-now problem and does not blame others for a host of past problems. It does not assume that the other person is to blame; instead it gives the other person the benefit of the doubt. Asking "What happened?" gives the other person a chance to explain. You avoid attacking the other person while you are angry. Indeed, one of the main points to this approach is to avoid becoming angry and blaming the other person. It is constructive, not destructive, because it builds toward a solution. The main point of the conversation is to find out what went wrong and how you can both fix it, rather than who was "wrong."

Summary

Effective team leaders know the importance of successful one-on-one meetings with team members. One-on-one meetings are essential for building consensus one on one, problem solving one on one, working through team member problems, reaching joint resolution on plans and decisions, and constructive confrontation when two people are having difficulty working together or communicating.

Good facilitation during one-on-one meetings helps leaders build trust and rapport with team members, aids in opening up communication and clearing up confusion, enhances team progress, and allows team members to develop leadership and facilitation skills. These skills are particularly useful for teams that are scattered geographically. A good deal of communication in distance teams is one on one, whether by phone or e-mail. In the next chapter, we will look at how team leaders can facilitate good cross-team and one-on-one communication when team members have little opportunity for face-to-face interaction.

8

Facilitating Communication of Distance Teams

In today's global world, teams are often spread out geographically. It is no longer a given that your team will all be in the same building, the same city, or even the same country. These "distance teams" provide special challenges to team leaders who strive to build team unity and coordinate the work of team members who may seldom see one another face to face.

What is expected of a geographically close team may not be appropriate for a distance team. However, just because teams are spread out does not mean that team leaders should give up on achieving the full benefits of teamwork. Even teams that are geographically close run into problems of not enough opportunities to meet face to face. One job of the leader of a distance team is to define the level of teamwork required to accomplish the work well and then to adapt team communications to build that level of teamwork. Facilitating teamwork at a distance requires the same clear team goals, frequent team communication, and consensus on importance decisions within the team.

The team leader of a distance team must encourage both face-to-face and electronic communication so that team members have ample opportunity to build relationships and to get the work done.

It is not enough to tell team members to communicate. An effective team leader models effective long distance communication and works with team members to determine what they should communicate, how frequently, and in what mode. The team leader can model the type of communication he or she thinks will benefit the group.

Rather than just assume that team members will communicate adequately by telephone and e-mail, it makes sense to do some planning for how team members and the team leader will communicate. For example, it may or may not be beneficial for team members to send weekly reports to one another via e-mail. The team may determine better ways to keep one another informed.

Team leaders and members should discuss the advantages and disadvantages of electronic and phone communication and determine the best ways for their team to correspond. Several things should be considered: the type of team, the degree of interdependence the work calls for, the frequency of face-to-face meetings, the nature of the work, and the time constraints faced by team members.

For a team to develop, build unity and strength, and realize the productivity that can come from effective teamwork, team members must work together. It is easy for members of distance teams to fall into the habit of little or no communication other than reports required by management. Each team member then becomes an island unto himself or herself. This leaves the team vulnerable to miscommunication, poor quality of work, missed deadlines, lack of cohesiveness, inefficiencies, and disaffected team members. Distance teams simply have to develop strong habits of communication via e-mail, telephone, and teleconferences.

Teams should be aware of the disadvantages of electronic distance communication and try to compensate for those negatives.

They should also be aware of the many advantages electronic communication presents and use this form of communication when possible to aid in building a strong team.

Communication Choices

Teams and team leaders have an array of communication tools at their disposal. Never before have there been so many methods to communicate with one another in a timely manner. Never before have there been so many avenues for people to put thoughts into words or into the minds of others. I am looking at the cover of a *New Yorker* magazine (May 29, 2000). Five people are sitting on a presumed commuter train. One is working at his laptop. Another is listening to a portable CD player. A woman is talking on her cell phone, while another woman is dictating into a small recording machine. Finally, one man is holding a toaster from which has just popped a piece of steaming hot toast. Everyone is plugged in, each doing his or her own thing. This is today's world. We can work, communicate, or function almost anywhere as long as we are plugged in.

Having so many choices about how to communicate can be an asset; it can also be a liability if people are not clear about what, when, and how to communicate. Today's challenge is how to communicate *effectively* and in a *timely* manner. Effective communication builds rapport and trust with others, while accomplishing necessary results.

Telephone

Generally speaking, the telephone is a strong substitute for face-to-face communication. Immediate dialogue is possible, and tone of voice, speed of speaking, and inflection all come together to convey much of the speaker's message. Disadvantages to the telephone for teamwork communication include the following:

- It can easily accommodate only small teams of two or three people at once.
- There is no common team documentation of what is agreed on.
- It can be difficult to find people at their telephones.
- It may be an unwanted interruption or inconvenient time for someone to talk.
- The pressure to finish a conversation may cause hasty, inadequately considered responses.

Some of these disadvantages can be overcome by facilitating a productive conversation as follows:

- Plan for the conversation or conference call ahead of time
- State agreed-on objectives for the conversation up front
- Have someone follow up with a written list of what was agreed on
- At the end of the conversation, review what was decided and check for common understanding and interpretation

These are all good facilitation techniques that can be adapted to the telephone. Especially important in a conference call is for someone to take the lead in structuring the conversation so that everyone participates.

Video

Video conferences, although sometimes tricky to set up because of time differences and availability of team members, can be a fairly good substitute for face-to-face meetings. Teams should be comfortable having a few video conferences a year and expect to accomplish quite a bit if the "meeting" is well-planned and facilitated. Flip charts can be used at a video conference in much the same way as in a face-to-face meeting. E-mail can also be used to document the group's ideas and decisions.

E-Mail

Because of its ease of use and its ability to reach immediately to all parts of the world, e-mail has become the much-preferred method of communication in most organizations today. When working recently with one large technical company, I noticed people racing back to their desks after every meeting to check their e-mail and send immediate replies. Some of these messages came from colleagues a few cubbies down the hall, colleagues they may not see in the course of a day, because most people were either in meetings or at their computers. This heavy reliance on e-mail has proliferated "instant communication," and people may be communicating much too frequently. As the day wears on, things change, and the message answered in the morning may need a different response by the afternoon. However, e-mail is a wonderful tool when its advantages and disadvantages are understood and when it is used in a productive way.

There are strong advantages to e-mail for some forms of communication. Teams can use e-mail to keep communication open and current. E-mail allows team members to do the following:

- Communicate with one another from almost anywhere at any time
- Virtually dialogue over an issue
- Conduct a mini-meeting

- Make minor changes in plans quickly and easily
- Reach one another in a timely fashion when telephoning is not feasible
- Send documents to one another with minimal effort
- Send copies to other people
- Communicate at length when face-to-face meetings are not possible
- Update team members who missed a meeting
- Communicate more effectively if they have trouble being understood when they speak English
- Communicate easily and frequently when they are separated geographically or when tracking one another down is difficult
- Send messages without interrupting someone else's work (as the telephone does)
- Solicit input from all team members fairly quickly
- Share information simultaneously with several people
- Quickly follow up a telephone conversation in writing

Teams should keep in mind that there are disadvantages to e-mail and institute other forms of communication to compensate for these disadvantages. Some disadvantages follow:

- It encourages too-frequent and too much communication, and thus can be inefficient.
- It is too easy for people to dump information on people who don't really need it.
- It becomes a convenient way for people to "show off" to others what they are doing and try to substantiate that they are working very hard.

- People receive too many e-mails and don't have time to respond thoughtfully to all of them.

- It lacks the synergy that arises from face-to-face brainstorming and idea sharing.

- It does not replace high-quality, face-to-face communication.

- Depending on the complexity of the message, a telephone conversation may be more adequate.

- For teams, certain important things are difficult to do by e-mail: brainstorm, hold an open group discussion, problem solve, reach consensus, and do project planning.

- The writer must be careful with wording, because the reader cannot pick up on other clues, such as voice inflection and body language.

- It lacks key components of building trust in relationships: body language, eye contact, and sharing experiences (eating lunch together, being in the same meeting, and so forth).

Simultaneous Multi-Electronic Communication

With so many options open for communication, teams can be creative by using various methods for different purposes and by using two or more methods at the same time. For example, it is possible to send out the agenda and objectives for a conference call via e-mail. During a conference call, call participants can use e-mail to relay or receive important information. Documentation of the telephone conference call can be done immediately and forwarded to all participants during or at the end of the call. Particularly sensitive decisions may require special wording or explanation, and these can be documented on e-mail while people are on the line for discussion. A group meeting face to face can bring others in via a conference call or video conference and relay documentation at the same time by e-mail.

Most facilitation processes—gathering inputs from everyone, brainstorming ideas, clarifying arrangements or solidifying decisions, determining action items, and so on—can be adapted to electronic communication. Keep in mind the importance of communicating clear, results-oriented objectives at the beginning of the electronic meeting, as well as precisely documenting decisions and action items at the end of the meeting.

Teams, and the business world in general, are beginning to take advantage of the Internet's capability for instant messaging, or synchronous chat. While working at their computers, team members can send messages to one another for instant receipt and timely response. Distance teams can use this facility to improve productivity. Some of the advantages of instant messaging follow:

- It allows for more timely communication.
- It helps avoid redundancies of effort.
- New information can be shared quickly with a number of people simultaneously.
- Team members can collaborate in real time.
- Team members can run things by one another for speedy feedback.
- It fosters a sense of camaraderie and "team."

Face to Face

The convenience of electronic communication does not diminish the importance of face-to-face meetings. Relying totally on electronic communication sacrifices the bonding and synergy that happen when team members meet and work face to face. Teams should use a combination of face-to-face meetings and electronic/ telephone communication. E-mail, video conferences, and conference calls can be used to push a team forward on plans, keep people informed, and work through simple problems and logistics. Meetings can be scheduled, confirmations made, and other plans determined without in-person contact. Simple problem solving and straightforward reporting and gathering of inputs are also possible electronically or by telephone.

However, there are situations in which teams should avoid using e-mail or other distance communication. Some issues call for face-to-face brainstorming, discussion, and planning. Some of these situations include reaching consensus on a difficult issue, solving complex problems, discussing involved or sensitive issues, setting long-term team goals, working out guidelines for team behavior, and resolving conflict. The synergy and trust building that must occur for these types of concerns require face-to-face group work, with all members and key stakeholders present, if possible. In fact, complex or sensitive issues that are addressed via electronic communication can easily be misinterpreted, blown out of proportion, or mishandled, causing problems for the team that may be difficult to unravel. Simply put, a team cannot really work together unless the members are together—at least some of the time. Being together in the presence of a facilitative leader usually increases understanding, fosters an atmosphere of comradeship and friendship, and brings critical concerns out in the open where they can be addressed by all. Group sessions that are well-facilitated allow people to speak freely and spontaneously, giving the added benefit of group energy (and synergy) that fuels the thinking process.

Tips for Managing Distance Teams

If you are building a team that is scattered geographically, there are several ways to compensate for the fact that members cannot simply walk across the hall to work with one another. First, it is highly important that team members become acquainted as soon as possible, preferably in a face-to-face orientation meeting. If such a meeting is not possible, you can facilitate team members becoming acquainted via e-mail. One way is by sending a few questions to the team (the same questions to everyone) and asking each team member to answer them and copy everyone in. The questions can be general and nonthreatening, with the intent to get to know one another. Encourage each team member to reply to teammates at least once. This way everyone has something to "say" to everyone else. You can ask the team members for any other ideas they have about how to become better acquainted via e-mail or the telephone. You can encourage team members to partner with one another on projects or problem solving. You can issue a brainstorming question to everyone and ask for replies and distribute these to everyone, asking people to build on others' ideas. Although much of the synergy of brainstorming is lost with this approach, it is not impossible to come up with fine ideas that team members can respond to. The final discussion is best done and the decision made when the group is together, but the initial idea generation can take place by e-mail.

If at all possible, bring the team together for a face-to-face meeting at least once or twice a year, if not quarterly. This will, of course, depend on the resources and needs of your individual team. Sometimes several teams can come together and work on single-team and multi-team concerns over a two- to five-day period. These face-to-face sessions are crucial to build trust and a sense of belonging. Because they are so important, these meetings should be well-planned and allow time for

- Becoming acquainted with one another
- Airing of concerns, questions, and issues
- Solidifying goals, plans, and decisions
- Reviewing how the team is doing
- Determining what needs to be done differently

Any face-to-face, participatory meeting requires facilitation and plenty of opportunity for people to interact and come to consensus. Allow some time for project planning so that team members can leave knowing what their individual tasks are. Timeframes and deadlines must be determined and agreed on. This is where the leader's facilitation skills come in. If the leader does not want to facilitate the session, he or she can bring in a facilitator and work with that person to have a facilitated meeting. Even if the team leader does not facilitate the session, he or she should take a facilitative role much of the time. This will encourage the involvement of everyone and show that each person's ideas and opinions are valued, heard, and considered. Team leaders must be careful not to dominate these meetings, but instead to listen, ask plenty of questions, and show support and empathy for team members' concerns.

Distance teams can keep in touch with a periodic, round-robin letter in which each team member puts forth information, issues, ideas, and questions. This should not be a formal "report," but an informal correspondence. Several questions could be answered by each team member, such as

- What is going well for you?
- What do you wish was going better?

- What milestones have you achieved, if any? Which milestones are you looking forward to?

- What do you need from other team members? From the team leader?

- How is the team doing in its work, its communication, and its sense of unity?

- How could the team function better?

Only one or two questions have to be addressed at a time. There should be no negative consequences for the responses, nor should team members expect that all their concerns will be resolved. The idea is to have an open forum. The team may want to honor confidentiality and not pass the e-mails on to anyone outside the team. One word of caution here: for this approach to work, team members *must* trust one another to keep their comments confidential. And, realistically speaking, team members may not choose to really open up when using this format. It is, however, a good way to touch base with one another in a semi-formal way.

Team members can decide when and how they will use these various means of keeping one another informed. The leader can stress to the team that electronic communication is not limited to data and reports but can be a way to socialize with one another as well. The team can decide what information it requires from each team member. At a subsequent meeting, team members can discuss how well their communication is working and decide what needs to be improved and how. The team leader does not have to be responsible for all of the team's communication. When the team is first formed, team members can contribute and implement ideas for communication. Later on, they can evaluate these ideas and make appropriate changes. The team leader should facilitate this process, ask the right questions of the group, see that the group's decisions are documented, and model the approach.

Electronic meetings should be kept simple and easy for all team members to "attend" and participate in. The basic principles of leading meetings and managing group work that are presented in Chapters Nine through Fourteen can be adapted and applied to distance meetings. For example, one question can be posed for everyone to respond to via e-mail or each member can submit a brief report and ask each team member to respond. The team leader can ask for information on a given project and have all team members copied in. A team member can call an "e-meeting," state a concern, and ask for ideas or help from other team members.

Summary

Just because there are numerous communication tools at everyone's disposal, team leaders should not assume that team members will communicate effectively. Each team and team leader must work out the best methods to connect with one another and determine which avenues of communication are most apt to initiate teamwork, build trust, and facilitate the team's work.

PART FOUR

Facilitating Team Meetings

Much of what is determined and initiated in teamwork is a result of effective team meetings. Facilitative leaders learn to structure group process for maximum participation, creativity, and consensus, while keeping the team's overall goals in mind.

Chapters Nine through Fourteen lay out the processes, skills, tasks, and behaviors needed to plan and lead a meeting that

- Involves everyone
- Maximizes the benefits of synergy
- Is focused and results-oriented
- Propels group members to action following the meeting
- Builds trust among group members
- Addresses concerns without becoming bogged down in them
- Builds team skills in the group

The skills presented in these chapters are fundamental facilitation and meeting planning skills. For further information and tools for facilitators, see *The Facilitator Excellence Handbook: Helping People Work Creatively and Productively Together* (Rees, 1998).

There are several other books on the market as well that help team leaders and facilitators structure group process so that maximum productivity is achieved. Some of these are mentioned in the References and Bibliography section at the end of this book.

9

Leading a Participative Team Meeting

Meetings are at the very heart of teamwork because of the important functions meetings perform. Much of what is accomplished in teams has a foundation in the team meeting. As is the case with democracy, meetings do not always work well, but they are the best way we have to get some things done. Those who live in the world of organizations know that these organizations are held together by face-to-face meetings and by quality long-distance communication.

Functions of Meetings

Meetings fill a deep human need. Human beings are a social species. In every organization and every human culture that we have a record of, people come together in small groups at regular and frequent intervals and in larger gatherings from time to time. Meetings give people a sense of belonging to the group. Members of groups that do not meet regularly usually do not feel a strong sense of belonging and do not take ownership for the success of the group.

A meeting performs several key functions better than any other communication device. For one thing, meetings define the team, the group, or the unit. Those who are present belong; those who are absent do not. Meetings are where the team revises, updates, and adds to what it knows as a team. A team creates its own pool of shared knowledge, experience, judgment, and folklore. As members exchange information and ideas they have acquired separately or in smaller groups, the team is strengthened. Meetings help each team member understand both the collective aim of the team and the way his or her own work, along with everyone else's, can contribute to the team's success.

Meetings are often the only time the team or group actually exists and works as a group and the only time when the team leader or manager is actually perceived as the group leader. In meetings, the team's goals, direction, and norms for operating are established. Meetings create in all present a commitment to the decisions that the team makes and the objectives that the team pursues. Meetings are the forum for gaining consensus, solving group problems, and making team decisions. Once something has been decided, even if you argued against it, your membership in the team entails an obligation to accept the decision. The decision-making authority of a meeting is of special importance for carrying out key actions, policies, and procedures.

Meetings are an important reflection of how the team members work together. In the meeting arena, the team leader can find out how individual members relate to one another and to the team. People find out who they are in relation to the team. They find out how much they are listened to, whether their ideas are supported, and what their responsibilities are as team members. The team meeting is a key place to see the team in action.

For a team or department to function smoothly, it generally needs to have meetings on a regular basis. Well-functioning teams, however, do not necessarily need to have a lot of meetings to do their work. In fact, the most effective teams do not always meet frequently. The meetings they do have, however, are productive and motivating.

Meetings, of course, serve functions besides those related to the team. Because of the complexity of organizations, goods, and services in American companies today, people simply *must* meet to share information and solve problems. The increased rate of change makes more meetings necessary. It is in the meeting setting where much information is shared, complexities are dealt with, misunderstandings are clarified, cross-functional issues and views are aired, and vital decisions are addressed.

It is becoming more important than ever for team leaders to have the skills and attitudes that make meetings productive. Issues that are not dealt with successfully in team meetings do not go away. *The meeting setting can be an efficient, productive, and beneficial way to get things done.* Unfortunately, many team leaders are simply not skilled at leading a productive meeting. In addition to lacking skills, they may also have an inappropriate team leadership style.

Leadership Style and Meetings

Generally speaking, team leaders run their meetings the same way they lead people. Those who are autocratic and directive in their approach to leading will probably do most of the talking and controlling at their meetings. In contrast, more democratic and collaborative team leaders will probably listen more at meetings and draw out the opinions and ideas of the team members. Leaders who tend to make up their minds before approaching others for an opinion may ask for the opinions of team members at meetings, but they will not pay much attention to those opinions. On the other hand, team leaders who seek input from others before making a decision are more likely to listen during team meetings.

Leadership meeting styles can be divided into these four categories:

- "Tell 'em, sell 'em" style
- Information-dissemination style
- Participative, "free-for-all" style
- Focused, participative style

"Tell 'Em, Sell 'Em" Style. The leader comes to the meeting with his or her mind made up and explains the decision to the others. With force of personality and influential argument, this type of leader presents his or her ideas to others, sometimes with forceful language and perhaps even passion. Meeting members are told how much their support is needed, and yet those members are given little opportunity to air their ideas, questions, or concerns. A few questions from meeting members may be answered throughout or at the end of the meeting, but little two-way communication is allowed.

Information-Dissemination Style. The leader uses meetings to inform everyone of what is going on in the department and in the larger organization. The leader, outsiders, and others in the group may give short or lengthy presentations to pass on vital (or not so vital) information. Meeting members may be given the opportunity to ask questions and discuss ideas, but the main focus of the meeting is the dissemination of information. Some people refer to these meetings as "information dumps."

Frequently, this type of meeting turns into an issue-raising session, during which all kinds of potential and real problems surface. But these problems are rarely resolved, because the meeting time is devoted to providing information. Meetings of this nature often become political platforms, where members vie for visibility and shoot holes in one another's information or projects.

Participative, "Free-for-All" Style. The leader gives meeting members more than ample time to participate and contribute. However, little progress is made toward solving problems or making decisions. This type of meeting is frustrating to those who need closure on issues or who must have decisions before they can progress with their projects. It is equally frustrating to those with busy schedules and under pressure to meet deadlines. Such a meeting seems like a waste of time.

Team leaders who use this style usually want input and participation from team members, but lack the desire or skills to bring issues to closure. Leaders of "participative free-for-alls" do not spell out clear objectives up front, and therefore consensus is difficult to reach in these meetings. The result: an interactive but meandering meeting where little is accomplished.

Focused, Participative Style. The leader encourages participation and involvement and focuses the group on clear meeting objectives. These objectives are agreed on by the group early in the meeting. This is the most desired style of meeting management if the meeting calls for group involvement and productivity. All group members become actively involved, and although the group may occasionally get off on a tangent, this type of leader soon refocuses the group on the defined objectives. This is the style of meeting leadership that this book addresses.

If team leaders want support and commitment from people, they must learn how to draw people out and collaborate with them, both individually and collectively. To maximize their human resources, leaders must bring out the experience and knowledge of everyone in the group, which a "focused, participative" approach can help them do. Leaders who become more facilitative in meetings will undoubtedly take a more facilitative approach to leadership in general.

What Goes Wrong in Meetings

"Not another meeting!" is a common lament in the hallowed halls of organizations today. The well-run, productive meeting seems to be the exception rather than the rule. In fact, so many things can go wrong at meetings that it is a wonder that some meetings do go well! Considering the amount of time wasted in meetings and their usual lack of productivity, it is surprising that such a small number of organizations focus on improving meetings.

The low productivity rate of business meetings puts a tremendous drain on our productivity as a nation. Not only are we losing precious time, a commodity that cannot be reproduced, but we are also spending money unproductively—money that could be put to better use.

Despite the problems with meetings, they are essential. The accelerating rate of change in all aspects of business and government has created the need for ad-hoc meetings, cross-functional task forces, meetings with customers, team meetings, and ongoing staff meetings. Much of the time spent in these meetings is used to communicate, understand, and plan for change.

The need for productivity in meetings has never been so great. To compete successfully, organizations must pursue all opportunities to save time and money. Because of the vast resources poured into meetings, they are a fitting target for productivity improvement.

Several problems are commonly associated with meetings today:

- Getting off the subject
- No clear objectives
- Poor attendance
- Too many distractions
- Lack of facilitation
- Not effective for making decisions
- Little pre-meeting orientation
- Canceled or postponed meetings

The Results of Poor Meeting Leadership

Several problems result from poor meeting leadership. Without a clear reason for meeting, it is natural for people to go off on tangents or for meeting time to be wasted on irrelevant discussion. Even if an agenda is published, it may not be enough to really focus the group on an objective or a meeting outcome. (Chapter Ten presents more on the problems with agendas and the importance of objectives.)

Without a clear meeting purpose, the leader will have trouble inviting the right people. Without a clear focus, people will be at the meeting for varying or unclear reasons. Their personal reasons will dominate, such as feelings of obligation, the desire for power and recognition, the need to address their own individual issues, or simply anxiety about being absent if something important is discussed.

Ineffective meeting processes also cause a host of problems. If participation is not structured and managed well, if conversation does not flow, and if people's ideas are not recorded and considered, the group will not be productive. A number of things can go wrong: group members are interrupted or discounted by others, the leader dominates the discussion, not enough time is set aside for meaningful participation, conflict and disagreements are not resolved, solutions are hastily arrived at with little reference to objective criteria. Decisions may be railroaded by dominant group members, with some people left out of the process altogether. No record of ideas is posted for use in discussing, planning, and deciding. Clarity and agreement about people's roles and responsibilities, or about the intended outcome of the meeting, are lacking. Any of these problems is enough to limit the meeting's effectiveness.

Without adequate meeting processes, the group is unlikely to achieve consensus or closure—even if it wants to do so. Closing on something that was not identified as a meeting objective in the first place is very difficult.

Once closure is reached—if it is—meeting leaders often fail to review exactly what was decided so that everyone understands. Sometimes in the push to end the meeting, follow-up actions are overlooked. And even when follow-up is planned, it is not always acted on. Sometimes decisions are reached without giving proper authority to those who must carry them out. Or closure may be postponed to another meeting but never be addressed again.

Disorganization in planning and running the meeting is largely responsible for the bad reputation of meetings. Disorganization seems to be the norm, rather than the exception. Here are some typical manifestations of meeting disorganization:

- The meeting is called and then canceled or postponed, sometimes several times.
- The meeting is held when a memo or phone call would have sufficed.
- Pre-meeting communication is inadequate or confusing.
- The meeting room is inadequate: too large, too small, too noisy, lacking needed materials and equipment.

- Record keeping during the meeting is nonexistent, disorganized, or poor.

- The wrong people are present, and the right people are absent.

- The meeting leader arrives late, leaves early, or assigns someone who is not prepared to lead.

- The meeting starts or ends late, time is wasted during the meeting, or the schedule is not adhered to.

Why do so many meetings seem to go nowhere? Why are most meetings a waste of everyone's time and effort? Why do people seldom leave a meeting feeling that they have accomplished something? There are three main reasons: (1) the purpose of the meeting is not clear; (2) the meeting progresses in a rather jumbled, haphazard fashion (or consists of one presentation after another); and (3) the meeting ends with little consensus or commitment. In short, meetings tend to have fuzzy beginnings, directionless middles, and endings with no closure.

At workshops on meeting facilitation that the author leads, participants identify what went wrong in meetings they have attended. Again and again, these same meeting problems—and others—come up. Most problems fall into four categories, all of which arise from unskilled, ineffective meeting leadership:

- No clear meeting objective or purpose
- Ineffective meeting processes
- No closure or follow-up
- Disorganization in planning or running the meeting

What Meetings Need

To be productive, meetings need clear objectives, a defined process, and closure on the objectives. Generally speaking, a successful participative meeting accomplishes two things: (1) something is resolved and (2) members leave the meeting committed to follow through on the decisions that are made.

The model for leading meetings is the same as the model for managing and leading teams:

> **L**ead with objectives
>
> **E**mpower to participate
>
> **A**im for consensus
>
> **D**irect the process

Lead with Objectives.   When clear meeting objectives are stated up front, the group's energy is directed toward achieving that outcome. The objectives then drive the *content* of the meeting. The facilitator must therefore see that the meeting begins with clear objectives. When team members are given, or help create, the objectives for the meeting, they are more able to contribute something of value and less likely to wander or be concerned with unrelated matters.

Empower to Participate.   To draw on the knowledge and experience of those present at a meeting, the leader must encourage active participation from all who are present. The L.E.A.D. model emphasizes participation and gives the leader responsibility for getting it.

Aim for Consensus.   For a meeting to be worthwhile, it must have an outcome, accomplish something. This is where consensus comes in. Without consensus and closure, a meeting has a feeling of futility; members leave wondering what they accomplished. Without the opportunity for consensus, members may feel either that nothing was accomplished or that they were railroaded into something on which they did not completely agree. A facilitator's ability to help a group reach consensus is critical to the meeting's success. Through the process of consensus, members "sign up" to support and carry out the decisions of the team.

Direct the Process. Just as important as clear objectives, participation, and consensus is the *process* of the meeting—how the meeting progresses. The process greatly influences the quality of the decisions made by the team. The meeting process also influences the commitment of each team member to the decisions made at the meeting. The L.E.A.D. model thus emphasizes the importance of process. However, many meeting leaders are so concerned with the meeting content that they ignore the process. For a meeting to be productive, it must involve all group members, encourage creativity and different viewpoints, and provide time for analyzing and solving difficult issues. A productive meeting must have a leader to guide its content, helping the group set clear meeting objectives, encouraging a high level of involvement and participation, and leading the group to consensus and closure.

Process Versus Content

It is important for meeting leaders to know the difference between the *process* of the meeting and the *content* of the meeting. Content is what the meeting is about, the subject or issue at hand; process is how the subject is dealt with. The content is what people usually have the most opinions about: what computer system to purchase, whether to redesign the product, what training program to implement, how to meet the quarterly profit goal, and so on. Meeting processes include discussions, presentations, pre-meeting committee or subgroup work, and flip charts used to record people's ideas. To test your understanding of the difference between process and content, take the quiz in Exhibit 9.1.

EXHIBIT 9.1. Quiz on Process Versus Content.

Instructions: Indicate after each item below whether it represents the *content* or the *process* of a meeting:

	Content	Process
1. Statement of the problem	✓	
2. Group discussion of the problem		✓
3. Information on a new procedure	✓	
4. Progress report	✓	
5. Breaking into small groups to discuss the advantages and disadvantages of a suggested procedure		✓
6. Idea contributed by one of the normally quieter group members		✓
7. Several side conversations going on at once		✓
8. Flip charts posted around the room with ideas the group generated		
a. The flip charts		✓
b. The ideas	✓	
9. Three alternatives to organizing a staff	✓	
10. Brainstorming session		✓

Note: Answers appear at the end of this chapter.

In most meetings, the process receives less attention than the content. The process is generally governed by a set of company or organization norms about how meetings should proceed. Some companies, for example, rely heavily on overhead slides and a presentation format. Others use flip charts with informal discussion. Some use a combination of both. One of the first and most important things to remember is this:

The process (how the meeting proceeds) is as important as the content (what the meeting is about).

If you refer to the list of things that go wrong at meetings presented earlier in this chapter, you will see that the majority of problems stem from ineffective meeting processes.

In summary, the content of a meeting is what the meeting is about; the process is the method used to accomplish the work of the meeting.

From Presentation to Facilitation

To understand more about meeting processes, think of a presentation-facilitation continuum (see Figure 9.1). In presentational meetings, the leader does most of the talking and group members participate very little. In facilitated meetings, the leader does little of the talking and group members participate most of the time.

The presenting style is a form of one-way communication, in which information is passed from the meeting leader to those attending the meeting. This type of meeting can be useful if the goal is to tell, sell, advocate, explain, inform, or announce. But some people question whether this type of meeting should be held at all. Information can be passed on through the written word, making a meeting unnecessary.

In contrast to the presentation, the facilitated meeting requires the involvement of group members. The reasons for this type of meeting are to listen, discover, uncover or solve problems, decide, create, and plan. A facilitated meeting could also be called a working session, where tasks are tackled and results are achieved.

A leader's style of running meetings can fall anywhere along the presentation-facilitation continuum. However, too many meetings lean toward the presentation side of the continuum, and too few fall into the facilitation category. Of course, the best style is the one that suits the purpose of the meeting. If the purpose of

FIGURE 9.1. Presenting Versus Facilitating: Leadership Styles.

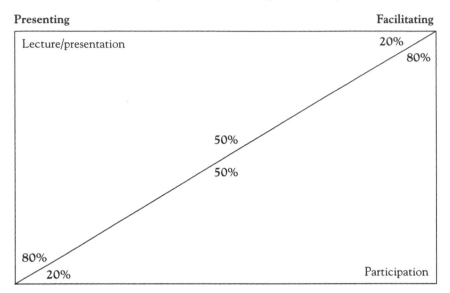

Presenting .... Facilitating

Presentation style
- Mostly one-way communication
- Presentation format
- Tell-and-sell approach
- Ideas presented and defended
- Suitable for passing on information
- Limits on group creativity

Facilitating style
- Multiple-way communication
- Participation format
- Problem-solving approach
- Ideas generated by group members
- Suitable for productive group work
- Maximization of group creativity

the meeting is simply to inform the group and answer questions, the presentation style is adequate. If, however, a great deal of input from group members is needed and ongoing commitment is important, a facilitating approach works best (see Figure 9.2).

The meeting leader's responsibility for the content and outcome of the meeting is greater on the presentation side of the continuum than on the facilitation side. On the facilitation side, group members share responsibility for the meeting outcome. The facilitator, however, is neutral on the outcome of the meeting—although he or she takes great responsibility for the meeting process. Therefore, moving along the continuum from presenta-

FIGURE 9.2. Presenting Versus Facilitating: Types of Meetings.

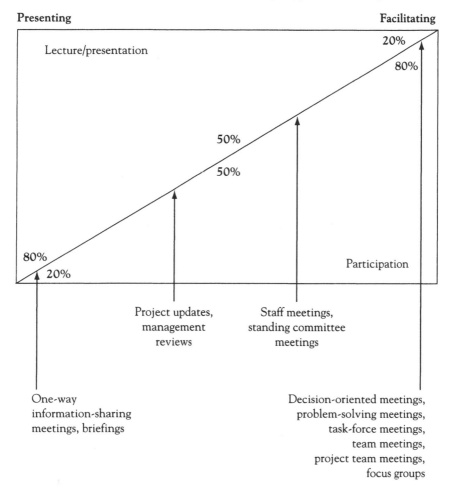

tion to facilitation is sometimes difficult. Team leaders often have a vested interest in the content of the meeting and have trouble remaining neutral.

Role of the Meeting Facilitator

A facilitator serves as a guide or a catalyst to help the group do its work. The facilitator seeks not to give an opinion on the meeting _content_ but simply to direct the _process_ so the best work of the group gets done. The facilitator provides the method and structure for a group to focus its energy and creativity on a particular task.

Although the role of the facilitator is similar to the neutral, third-party role of mediators and arbitrators, there is a major difference: mediators and arbitrators become involved in the content of a dispute, whereas a facilitator remains detached, unbiased, and neutral. A facilitator makes suggestions about how the group should proceed to accomplish its goals.

A facilitator must have knowledge of group processes and make certain that meeting participants are using the most efficient methods for accomplishing their task. When it comes to the content of the meeting, the facilitator remains nonevaluative.

Doyle and Straus (1976) describe the facilitator as a traffic cop directing the meeting's process. The facilitator provides rules or norms for the group and then monitors the group so it does not violate those norms. For example, if a group is brainstorming ideas to solve a problem, the facilitator may instruct the group that all ideas will be recorded and considered and that, in the initial stages of the brainstorming process, no one is to evaluate or discount any of the ideas. If someone tries to evaluate or discount an idea, the facilitator intervenes to remind the group of the rules.

A group that is used to being facilitated will begin to suggest its own processes and will police itself somewhat. However, groups that are new to facilitation need to be reminded from time to time about how to proceed.

One exception to the "rule" of remaining neutral on content is when a facilitator is conducting a training program or passing on important information. In these cases, the facilitator may play a dual role: content expert (presenter) and process expert (facilitator). A skilled trainer learns when to teach or be the content expert, and when to step back and simply facilitate a discussion or group exercise. The facilitator-trainer judiciously chooses when to encourage the group to discover, discuss, and decide on its own. A facilitator-trainer can actually lead a training session without being the content expert, as long as there is someone present who can be a content resource.

There is really no right way to facilitate, no prescribed facilitator approach or style. Much depends on the facilitator's personality, the situation, the nature of individuals in the group, and certainly the dynamics of that particular combination of people. No two facilitations are alike, because the very nature of facilitation encourages ongoing adaptation to the group and to the task at hand.

Facilitators draw from a tool bag of techniques when planning and leading a meeting. Here are some of the things skilled facilitators do:

- Maintain a climate conducive to participating, listening, understanding, learning, and creating

- Listen actively

- Help the group establish and accomplish its own objectives

- Provide structure and guidance to increase the likelihood that objectives will be accomplished

- Keep the group focused on its objectives

- Encourage dialogue and interaction among participants

- Suggest and direct processes that empower and mobilize the group to do its work

- Encourage the group to evaluate its own progress or development

- Capitalize on differences among group members for the common good of the group

- Remain neutral on content and be active in suggesting and directing the process

- Protect group members and their ideas from being attacked or ignored

- Use facilitation skills to tap the group's reservoir of knowledge, experience, and creativity

- Sort, organize, and summarize group inputs or get the group to do so

- Help the group move to healthy consensus, define and commit to the next steps, and reach timely closure

The objective, process-oriented role of the facilitator is critical. Someone needs to guide the process of the meeting. But facilitating and contributing to the meeting at the same time require concentrated effort.

Most people at a meeting, including the group leader, are interested in the content or outcome and therefore have trouble being objective. Meeting members have a lot to do just to function as effective meeting participants. They must think through their ideas and express them so that others will understand and consider them. They must hear and consider the ideas of others.

Meeting members may also have to deal with tensions resulting from "hidden agendas"—personal issues they may want to address. Some may be acutely aware of these agendas but may not feel comfortable addressing them. Others may not even be aware of their own hidden agendas, which nevertheless cloud the picture for them. Whether conscious or subconscious, hidden agendas often influence the meeting. They are usually expressed or dealt with in indirect—and often unhealthy—ways.

To further complicate the process, a meeting often becomes a place where people pursue interpersonal and political issues or vie for visibility. Most group members have trouble putting personal and political issues aside during a meeting. Someone needs to keep the group on track. The facilitator can help discover and then dilute or refocus hidden agendas. A skilled facilitator will balance such digressions with the group's objective.

The facilitator's role is to provide objectivity and identify and explain processes that will help the group do its work. Must the facilitator therefore be someone from outside the group? Is it impossible for the team leader to achieve this neutral role? Not necessarily. However, the facilitator must be someone who can—and will—remain neutral during the meeting, someone who will direct the process fairly. This is the challenge to the meeting leader: to be neutral, to empower others to get the work done.

non member facilitator — good idea

Summary

To lead a participative meeting, team leaders need the following skills:

- Designing and planning a meeting
- Focusing the meeting
- Encouraging participation
- Recording people's ideas
- Managing the group process
- Organizing, connecting, and summarizing data
- Bringing the group to consensus and closure

These skills will be covered in the next few chapters.

A facilitator should not only have these skills but also be able to present and develop a topic, because occasionally he or she needs to put on a "content hat" and explain something or pass on information.

Answers to Quiz in Exhibit 9.1. Items 1, 3, 4, 8b, and 9 represent the *content* of a meeting; the rest represent the *process* of a meeting.

10

Planning and Focusing the Meeting

Simply speaking, objectives are focused; agendas are not. Objectives define the desired outcome of the meeting; agendas define only the topics to be covered. Objectives give teams and groups something to strive for; agendas give them something to endure. Objectives call for active participation; agendas permit passivity.

Why Agendas Do Not Work and Objectives Do

Most people agree that one of the most important ingredients of a meeting is an "agenda" and that a meeting is successful if the agenda is adhered to and completed. Without a doubt, a meeting with an agenda that serves as a focal point is more successful than a meeting that rambles on and on without an agenda or a time schedule.

However, an agenda is not enough. It usually includes only a list of topics to be covered, a time schedule, and the name of the presenter for each item. A typical agenda might look like this:

9:00	Update on the Colby Project	Tom
9:30	The July 7–8 Offsite	Jean
10:00	Third-Quarter Report	Bob
10:30	Open Agenda	
11:00	Adjourn	

The dangers lurking in an agenda like this are many. First, it provides no clearly stated objectives for the meeting. What is the purpose of the meeting? For each agenda item, what will be accomplished? What do the members expect to accomplish? How will they know the meeting was successful? Because the desired outcome is not spelled out, the leader will have trouble keeping the group on track. When group members take off on tangents, the leader will have no stated purpose to bring them back to.

A second danger with agendas like the one above is that the topics it lists may not be the main concern of the group. Unless group members come up with the agenda, which does not usually happen, they are not likely to be very interested in it.

Third, using agendas and omitting objectives can lead to three unproductive developments:

- A series of long-winded, boring presentations
- Several free-for-all discussions going nowhere
- A combination of boring presentations and free-for-all discussions

A fourth problem with agendas is their excessive flexibility. A safe guess is that 50 percent or more of meetings with agendas never adhere to the set schedules. Agenda items are moved around, added, and deleted; people come and go; someone takes more than the allotted time; the group becomes sidetracked or bogged down on one agenda item. Such a meeting suffers a sense of disorder and a loss of direction, and people feel that it will just go on and on with no defined stopping point.

The way to avoid such problems is to establish one or more clearly stated objectives for the meeting. An <u>agenda can then</u> be <u>created to support the objectives</u>. Instead of a list of topics, the agenda becomes a flow of activities that the team or group will take part in to accomplish the objective.

Productive agenda

A sample meeting objective with its supporting agenda might look like this:

> Our objective for today's meeting is to decide which one of the three alternative database management systems best meets our established criteria. The agenda for the meeting will be:
>
> 9:00   Review criteria. <u>Make</u> necessary changes.
> 9:30   <u>Discuss</u> pros and cons of each system in relation to criteria.
> 10:00 <u>Plot</u> decision grid. <u>Rank</u> choices.
> 10:30 <u>Discuss</u> top-ranked choice. <u>Weigh</u> against criteria. <u>Decide</u> on system.

Verbs

Another way of publishing the agenda is to <u>leave off the times</u>, showing only the approximate length of the meeting:

Agenda
September 27
9:00–10:30
- Review criteria. Make necessary changes.
- Discuss pros and cons of each system in relation to criteria.
- Plot decision grid. Rank choices.
- Discuss and decide.

When team leaders become comfortable with leaving decisions to the group and group members get used to facilitation processes, the objectives and agenda can be created by the group before the meeting begins. This practice is an excellent way to strengthen the group and increase the likelihood that the meeting will be productive. Everyone will have a say not only in the goal for the meeting but also in how the meeting will proceed.

Objectives: The Driving Force of a Good Meeting

Before calling a meeting, the most important question to ask is "What will this meeting achieve?" This question can be answered before the meeting by the leader, who can also consider the following questions: "What do we need to accomplish at this meeting?" "What would happen if we didn't have this meeting?" "When the meeting is over, how will we know it was successful?" Unless the need for the meeting is very clear, it may be a waste of everyone's time.

The meeting's objective leads to additional considerations:

- *Is the meeting necessary?* Can the objective be accomplished more efficiently in another way?

- *Who should attend the meeting?* Those who have information related to the objective or who will be involved in authorizing or implementing the objective need to be at the meeting. Others do not.

- *When should the meeting be held? How long do we need?* Both questions should be answered with the meeting objective in mind.

- *Where should the meeting be held?* What environment and atmosphere does the meeting call for?

- *Is any pre-meeting work necessary?* Will the group accomplish more if members prepare for the meeting ahead of time? What should members bring to the meeting?

- *What processes will accomplish the objective?* Brainstorming? A problem-solving model? Small-group work? An informative presentation? A short training session? Prioritizing?

- *What adjustments need to be made during the meeting?* As the meeting progresses, is the group making progress toward its objective, or does it need to do something differently?

- *Was the meeting successful?* Did the group achieve what it set out to achieve? If not, why not? How might the next meeting be improved?

Clear objectives are probably the most important element of a productive meeting. They help the leader to maintain control while encouraging maximum participation. Objectives focus the group, drive the outcome, and serve as a measure of performance and productivity.

Skilled facilitators have discovered that clarifying and posting meeting objectives early in the meeting is a powerful way to focus the group, involve people, and direct the meeting toward consensus. Also, they have learned that the wording of the objectives is important: objectives need to be clear, realistic, focused, and measurable. The wording *is* the objective.

Writing Meeting Objectives

Writing out the objectives for a meeting helps everyone understand its purpose. When the objectives are also posted where they can be seen during the meeting, they keep the group focused.

It is helpful to think of a meeting objective as having three ingredients: an *action*, an *outcome*, and *qualifiers* (if necessary).

Actions that groups can accomplish in a meeting are described by such words as *plan, develop, decide, determine, generate, identify, recommend, list, prioritize, solve, resolve,* and the like. Start the objective with an action word that describes what the group will do during the meeting, something that can be observed. For example, you can specify whether a group is to *list* something or *decide* something or *plan* something.

Avoid using action words that are vague or that do not lend themselves to clear results. For example, you can say the objective is to discuss something, but simply discussing something at a meeting does not produce much of a result. Words like *discuss, understand, update,* and *explore* do not describe clear outcomes. Replace them with more results-oriented words. Instead of "Discuss the pros and cons of our new telephone system," try "Decide how to improve the use of our new telephone system." Instead of "Discuss how to improve customer service," try "Generate a list of ideas that will improve customer service and select the top two or three for immediate implementation."

Each of the suggested objectives has two key ingredients: an *action* and an *outcome*. The action describes what the members will be doing at the meeting. The outcome tells what the product or result of that action will be. For example, in "Decide how to improve the use of our new telephone system," the action is *decide*. The outcome is *how to improve the use of our new telephone system.* The other example, "Generate a list of ideas that will improve customer service and select the top two or three for immediate implementation," specifies two actions: *generate* and *select*. The outcome of the meeting will be two or three ideas that will be implemented immediately. When members leave the meeting, they will have made specific decisions about what they are going to do to improve customer service.

Compare these meeting objectives to the sort of vague agenda items that are more typical. The previous two objectives might have been phrased this way on an agenda: (1) "discussion of the new telephone system" and (2) "how to improve our customer service."

Objectives usually need some additional words to put them in clear focus for the meeting. These words, called *qualifiers,* further describe the objective and set important parameters, such as time frames. For example, one of the previous objectives includes several qualifiers (noted here in italics): "Generate a list of ideas *that will improve customer service* and select *the top two or three for immediate implementation.*" These qualifiers specify that the ideas have to improve customer service, that the group has to select the top two or three (not just one and not all of them), and that the two or three ideas that are selected have to be implemented immediately. An objective does not necessarily need this many qualifiers, but the more qualifiers you include, the clearer and more focused the objective will be. A good question to ask is whether you have included enough qualifiers to focus the group.

In summary, remember that a meeting objective must have an action, an outcome, and the qualifiers necessary to focus the group. Check also to see that your objective describes a realistic accomplishment for that meeting.

Managing Meeting Flow

Once the meeting objectives have been decided and agreed on, the next step is to decide on the flow of meeting activities. This flow could be called the meeting "agenda." Figuring out how to lay out the meeting becomes easier with experience as a facilitator. An understanding of group process is important. What activity will start the group rolling? What is the best process to use to accomplish the objective? (Several processes for helping groups to come to consensus are described in Chapter Fourteen.) Encouraging active participation and involvement is one skill; planning and structuring the meeting so participation will be productive is another.

The first step is to decide how you will focus the group on the purpose of the meeting. (Several ways to bring focus to a meeting are presented later in this chapter). The second step is to find a way to get everyone participating as soon as possible (see Chapter Eleven). One technique is to have some kind of introductory activity that will require everyone's input, so dominant members will not take over right at the beginning of the meeting. The third step is to plan the group processes you will use to accomplish the objective. (Chapter Fourteen describes several, such as brainstorming and clustering.) Finally, plan how you will close the meeting. What activity will you use to reach closure and to decide on the next steps the group must take? The meeting should not end until group members feel they can support the group's decision, clearly understand just what that decision is, and identify action steps and responsibilities for carrying out that decision.

When planning a meeting, remember that participation takes time. Leave plenty of time for each activity, and anticipate more discussion and involvement, rather than less. Build in time for letting the group stray off the topic a bit, as digressions sometimes help people get a grip on the real problem. In the long run, time spent ensuring participation saves time. People will leave the meeting with more commitment to the group's decision and a clearer picture of what has to be done.

Planning for Participation

Here are some things to remember when planning a meeting:

- Start with an activity that includes everyone. Choose something easy for people to do or talk about, something that relates to the work at hand.

- If presentations are necessary, keep them short and to the point. Give people ample time following each presentation to comment and ask questions.

- Try to structure meetings so group members are talking 80 to 90 percent of the time. The leader-facilitator should listen, record, and suggest processes. Team members should do the thinking, talking, deciding, and so on.

- Vary activities to include some small-group or subgroup work. Let people work in pairs or in subgroups of three or four and then come back to the larger group to share their ideas or report their findings. Avoid subgroup work, however, at the beginning and end of the meeting. Generally, it is best to start and end with all group members together.

- Decide before the meeting how you will organize data on flip charts or other media. Think ahead about problems that may arise in organizing the data and how you might deal with them. For example, if you are going to do brain-storming, the group will probably come up with a long list of ideas. You may want to leave a space before each idea so you can label it later.

- Anticipate that stray issues will come up, and decide ahead of time how you will handle them. One way is to appoint someone at the beginning of the meeting to record these ideas and bring them to the next meeting. Another way is to have a flip chart available so you can record the ideas as they come up. You can consult the group members at the end of the meeting about how they want to handle the extra ideas.

Chapter Eleven presents some additional methods for fostering participation.

Preparing Notification Memos and Prework

When planning the meeting, ask yourself what group members can do prior to the meeting to make it more productive. The tasks you come up with constitute the meeting prework. *Caution:* Prework that group members consider too time-consuming, unclear, or unimportant probably will not be done. When planning the meeting, you must therefore also ask, "How likely is it that people will complete the prework? Is the prework really necessary?"

A group that meets regularly may not need a pre-meeting notification memo. The members may have agreed on the prework and meeting objectives at the end of the previous meeting. But when a notification memo does need to be distributed, use the opportunity to clearly state the objectives for the meeting. If the group is going to decide its own objectives at the beginning of the meeting, the pre-meeting memo might read, "We will start by determining what we want to accomplish during the meeting."

Focusing a Meeting

The most productive groups clearly understand why they are meeting and what they must accomplish. There are several ways to help group members focus on their objective:

- Use the *pre-meeting memo* to communicate the meeting objectives and let people know what to expect.

- Read and post the *objectives* at the meeting for all to see and refer to. If the group participates in creating its objectives for the meeting, write and post these objectives after the group has finalized them.

- Use the meeting *agenda* to let people know what activities to expect and about how long each will take. Then they can spend more energy participating and less energy wondering what is going to happen next or when the meeting will be over.

- At the beginning of the meeting, use an *activity that includes everyone*. Such an activity will reinforce the idea that everyone's contribution is valued and will help everyone focus on the meeting.

- When appropriate, set *general rules or norms* for the meeting. The roles people will play in the meeting may also need to be defined. For example, will the group's leader be a participant in the meeting or the facilitator? Who will record the group's ideas and decisions? What role will guests or others play? Explicit rules and roles are especially helpful if those attending the meeting are not used to meeting together or if the way the group has been operating is changing.

- Sometimes it is appropriate and valuable to ascertain the *expectations of group members* at the beginning. The facilitator then knows where people are coming from and can either adjust the meeting to meet their expectations or clarify up front that it will not be possible to meet them. One technique that works is to ask, "Given our objectives for today, what expectations do you have for this meeting?" Give everyone a chance to think and respond, and record the comments; after all expectations have been expressed, address each one briefly. This technique helps people understand the intent of the meeting and focus on the objective at hand. It <u>is especially useful for long, difficult meetings and meetings</u> to which people are likely to bring <u>a lot of issues, concerns, and hidden agendas.</u>

Summary

Use these techniques to focus your meetings, and they will become more participative and productive:

- Write results-oriented meeting objectives and post them for all to see; get agreement from the group that these are the appropriate objectives and use them throughout the meeting to keep people focused and productive

- Use the agenda to support these results-oriented objectives

- Design a meeting flow that encourages and allows time for active participation from all participants

- Assign simple, clearly explained prework for the meeting, if this will make the meeting more productive

- At the beginning of the meeting, lead an activity that includes everyone, to get every team member contributing right away

- Set, or have the team set, meeting norms that will ensure participation, creativity, and productivity

11

Encouraging Participation

One of the facilitator's key roles is to create an atmosphere of openness and trust, to encourage people to speak up and contribute. Several techniques will either encourage or discourage participation in a group setting. Facilitators need to be keenly aware of what these are and use them appropriately to achieve a balance of participation. They include what the facilitator says, what the facilitator does, how the facilitator listens, how the activities are structured, and the room environment and setup. What the facilitator says can be referred to as *verbal* techniques; what the facilitator does can be referred to as *nonverbal* techniques. These verbal and nonverbal techniques are critical to good facilitation.

Verbal Techniques: What to Say

These are some of the most important verbal techniques:

- Ask open-ended questions
- Phrase requests to encourage more responses
- Acknowledge and positively respond to contributions made by participants
- Ask for more specifics or examples

- Redirect questions or comments to other members of the group
- Encourage nonvocal participants to participate
- Ask for and encourage different points of view
- Paraphrase for clarity and understanding
- Avoid stating an opinion or interjecting ideas while facilitating
- Refer to contributions people have made

Asking an Open-Ended Question. Asking people a question that cannot be answered with "yes" or "no" is one of the easiest, most basic techniques for drawing people out. An open-ended question simply asks for information, an idea, a reaction, or an opinion. Open-ended questions usually begin with "What," "How," "Who," or "Why." Some examples are

- "What is your reaction to that?"
- "What, in your opinion, is the best way to. . . ?"
- "What suggestions do you have to improve the way we. . .?"
- "How can we improve the way we handle customer complaints?"
- "What alternatives do we have?"
- "Why do you think we are having problems with. . . ?"

Closed-ended, or directive, questions are those that can be answered with "yes" or "no" or that direct the respondent to specific answers. They begin with such phrases as "Do you," "Are you," "Is that," "Does that," and "Isn't it better to." This type of question is useful in certain situations, but not very effective for drawing on the synergy and expertise of a group. A good facilitator usually avoids closed-ended questions. They are effective, however, if the facilitator wants to wrap up a topic and move on. They also help people to agree on specifics: "Are we in agreement, then, that. . . ?" "Then is this the best alternative?"

Using Requests to Encourage More Responses. Another important facilitator technique for encouraging participation is to ask people to supply more information or to expand on an idea. These types of requests usually begin with words or phrases such as "Describe," "Tell us," and "Explain." Here are some examples:

- "Describe the process you used"

- "Tell us more about that"

- "Explain the difference between the two systems"

Positively Responding to Contributions Made by Participants. A little positive reinforcement goes a long way; it can be overdone. The trick is to be genuine without being repetitive or distracting. Without any positive reinforcement at all, however, especially if the meeting leader appears serious and determined, meeting participants may not feel encouraged to open up or to speak their minds.

Positive reinforcement can be accomplished with such comments as "Thank you," "Good point," "That's a new idea," "That's interesting," or "Let's write that down." To build rapport and personalize the meeting, it also helps to occasionally use the name of the participant: "Thank you for bringing that out, Jim" or "Thank you, Sue; that's a point we hadn't considered yet."

A word of caution is appropriate here. Using this technique too frequently lessens its effect. A facilitator should not comment after every input, but just often enough to encourage people to contribute. The facilitator must strike a balance between being unresponsive and being overly responsive. Other ways to positively reinforce contributions are discussed in this chapter under "Nonverbal Techniques: What to Do."

Asking for More Specifics or Examples. When open-ended questions and comments that encourage more responses do not bring out enough specifics or when someone uses platitudes or generalizations that do not further people's understanding of the topic, the facilitator can move the discussion along by asking for specifics, for example:

- "Could you be a bit more specific?"
- "Can you go further into that?"
- "What do you mean by. . . ?"
- "Can you help us out by giving an example?"

Redirecting Questions or Comments to Other Members of the Group. This powerful and much-underused technique encourages dialogue among participants and draws attention away from the facilitator. For example, when asked a question by one of the participants, the facilitator might say something like "What do the rest of you think about that?" or "Someone here must have a response to that" or "I'd like to throw that question out to the whole group; what do some of you think?" Another appropriate use of this technique is when a group member comments on something said earlier by another member. The facilitator may then say something like "That relates to something Jim said earlier about. . . . Jim, what is your response?"

Although at times participants might find this technique annoying, redirecting questions or comments at the appropriate time puts responsibility for the discussion on the participants' shoulders, not on the meeting leader's. It also keeps the dialogue going and knits participants together as a team. The leader who uses it is maintaining a balance of participation and ensuring that the team members respect and build on one another's ideas. Once group members become used to this technique, they may respond on their own if the facilitator just remains silent. Eventually they will direct their comments to one another instead of to the facilitator.

Encouraging Nonvocal Participants to Participate. It is important to try to balance participation by drawing out even the quietest group members. The key is for the facilitator to be aware of who is participating and who is not. Someone who has not contributed may then be drawn out in a direct way: "Bill, any reaction to this?" or "Joan, we haven't heard from you yet; what do you think?"

If the facilitator suspects that the person's mind has wandered and that he or she may be caught by surprise, then the facilitator can repeat enough of the topic to enable the person to respond. For example: "Sue, it's been a while since we heard from you. What do you think of the XYZ alternative?"

Another technique is to ask each person separately for a response to the same question. Used sparingly, this is a fine way to balance participation. Frequently, the quieter person is shy or does not want to interrupt others or is uncertain about when to jump in. In some cultures, such as the Japanese culture, it is considered rude to interrupt another person. But in many American meetings, the talking does not stop long enough for someone to contribute in a "polite" way. As a result, Japanese often appear quiet even though they have contributions to make. A knowledgeable and sensitive facilitator will find ways to give people from all cultures the opportunity to speak up.

Asking For and Encouraging Different Points of View. When group members are all in agreement and no different viewpoints have been expressed, several things may be wrong. Some people may be holding back for fear of recrimination. Or the group may be intent on coming to a quick solution so it can get on with other things. People who have been together as a team for some time may also start to think alike. This phenomenon, called "groupthink," inhibits creative problem solving. Of course, another possible reason for a lack of disagreement is that there really is little disagreement.

Lack of divergent viewpoints is a signal to the facilitator to intervene. When a group seems ready to agree before sufficient testing or development of ideas has taken place, the facilitator must open up additional discussion and consideration: "We have discussed only one or two viewpoints. Are there some other points of view on this subject?" or "Is there something we haven't thought of?" or "Can anyone think of a way this doesn't fit?"

If no one responds, the facilitator can try switching positions, throwing out a different view for consideration: "What about the view that. . . ?" Facilitators should use this technique sparingly, because switching positions too often may make them appear too involved in the content or even manipulative. This technique should be used to help, not hinder, the productive work of the group. Fortunately, a group that is used to being facilitated will not need this technique very often.

Paraphrasing for Clarity and Understanding. This is a good technique for facilitators who want to check their understanding of what another person has said or who want to make sure that everyone in the room has a clear idea of what is being said. For example: "Let's see, Pete. If I understand correctly, you are saying. . . ."

Avoiding Stating an Opinion or Interjecting Ideas While Facilitating. Paraphrasing too frequently can be risky, especially if it gives group members the impression that the facilitator is rephrasing comments to make them sound better or to have the last word. Participants will become demoralized if they hear the message that their words are not good enough or if they feel that the discussion centers too much around the facilitator. Yielding to the temptation to comment on the proceedings discourages valuable interaction among the other participants, causing good thoughts to be lost and time to be wasted.

Referring to Contributions People Have Made. When doing so will help the group be clear about its work, the facilitator may wish to relate one person's comment to another. For example, when two or three people are saying similar things, the facilitator may point out, "That sounds like what Yoshi said earlier about. . . ." Cross-references like these help the group reach consensus. They also encourage and reward participation, showing that the facilitator is really listening to what people are saying.

Nonverbal Techniques: What to Do

Although harder to pinpoint than verbal techniques, nonverbal techniques (what a facilitator does) are just as important.

In fact, what one does when facilitating must match what one says. If it does not, it will give mixed messages and create an atmosphere of distrust. For example, if the facilitator asks an open-ended question but moves right into the next sentence without waiting for an answer, he or she is telling people that there is really no expectation for them to respond. They will get the message that the facilitator does not want their contributions, and they will stop participating.

The facilitator's nonverbal behavior can let participants know that he or she is attentive, interested in their ideas, and willing to let them proceed without interference. Some important nonverbal behaviors are

- Attentiveness
- Voice and facial expressions
- Silence
- Movement and position in the room

Attentiveness. The most important rule of facilitation is to pay attention to the person who is talking. A facilitator who does not listen well hinders the group's productivity. Establishing good eye contact with the person speaking, relaxing posture, and turning toward the speaker are all good ways to foster attention. A few head nods to show understanding will encourage the speaker to continue. Unless a facilitator needs to cut off a long-winded person, he or she should not interrupt and should also avoid distracting movements (rattling keys, playing with a pen, and so on) and doing other things while people are speaking. One possible exception is writing the group's ideas on a flip chart. Although turning away to write on a flip chart may seem to detract from attentiveness, the act of recording someone's idea is usually powerful enough to make up for the loss of eye contact.

Voice and Facial Expressions. A facilitator's voice and facial expressions may also enhance or detract from his or her effectiveness. A voice that encourages participation is clear but not overpowering; it displays confidence and enthusiasm. The volume of the voice is loud enough for all to hear, projecting to the back of the room. Facial expressions similarly affect the mood of the group. A serious or deadpan face may bring down its energy level. Frowns tend to discourage participation. Smiles usually encourage and relax people, but too much smiling may discredit the facilitator and distract participants.

Silence. Because we are so often concerned with what we say, we may neglect what we do not say. Silence is a critical tool of a good facilitator and a much-forgotten art. Good listeners know when to pause, wait, and say nothing, and they regularly put this knowledge to use. It is especially important to pause after asking a question. This gives people time to think of their responses; a pause will indicate that a facilitator really wants to hear what they have to say. Try not to get anxious and restate or rephrase the question. A good rule of thumb is to wait about ten to twelve seconds. (Usually someone will respond after seven to ten seconds.) Those seconds will seem like a long time, but they will pass quickly for the people who are thinking about possible responses. If nobody responds after ten to twelve seconds, then ask the question again, rephrase it, or move on.

Using silence wisely makes the group responsible for its own progress. After someone has responded to a question, be silent so participants can respond to one another; let the group carry on by itself. Above all, do not always insist on having the last word. A good facilitator does not want to be the focal point, but wants the others to interact.

Movement and Position in the Room. The way the facilitator moves around the room can affect participation. Generally speaking, standing fixed in one spot with hands and arms rigidly in some position (straight down, folded, or in pockets) is not a good idea. Stiffness conveys tenseness and nervousness. It is better to move about in a relaxed manner or to sit down than it is to stand in one spot. If the chairs in the room are arranged in a U-shaped config-uration, the facilitator might occasionally move closer to the par-ticipants who are sitting at the base of the U. Moving closer to people naturally draws them into the conversation. Another tech-nique is to move behind the participants, to the back of the room outside the U, and let the group carry on by itself. Use this tech-nique after a discussion has started. Sitting down where you can see group members but they cannot see you also works well. Some-times sitting down and joining the group works, but other times you may lose control of the group or lose your credibility. Sitting down for too long may also cause the group to be too relaxed and lose energy. This technique usually works best when the team is engaged in active discussion and the members have a lot of energy and enthusiasm for their topic.

Managing the Environment

Some room environments discourage participation, so whenever possible set up the room to encourage dialogue and interaction. Arrange tables and chairs so people can see one another. Position the flip chart and the overhead projection screen so they are visi-ble to everyone. If you will be posting sheets of paper from a flip chart, make sure you have adequate room to hang them where people can see them.

Room layouts that are U-shaped or modifications of that shape are best (see Figure 11.1). Everyone can see almost everyone else and the visuals at the front of the room. The facilitator can stand, sit, or move in and out of the U. A conference table setup is second best. Group members can still see one another, but the facilitator

FIGURE 11.1. Meeting-Room Layouts.

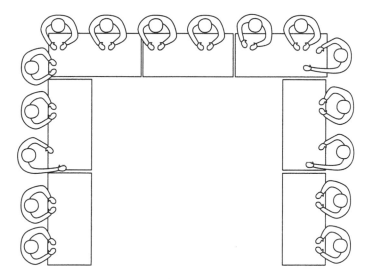

U-shaped setup

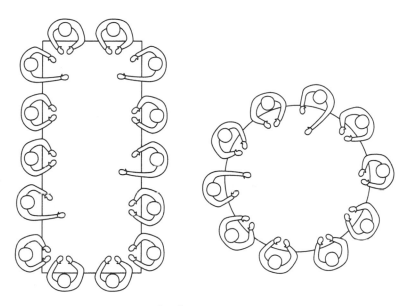

Conference setups

and the visuals may not be so visible to everyone at the table. Refreshments are best placed at the back of the room; they become distracting when placed at the front of the room.

A meeting room should have adequate space, but participants should not feel dwarfed. For example, members of a new team meeting for the first time in a large conference room may feel small and insignificant in such a large space. They may not participate as much as they would in a smaller room. If you must use a large room, try blocking off a smaller space with a screen, charts, or other barriers to create the feeling of a more intimate space.

For meetings that call for small groups to go off and work together, breakout rooms or spaces are important. They give small groups privacy and quiet and also give people a change of scenery. In fact, a change of scenery is a desirable break in any long meeting. Let people move around or work in a different area. If you cannot let them change rooms, assemble them into subgroups or pairs within the room.

Other considerations for choosing a meeting room are temperature, air, noise, and view. Aim to minimize distractions, discomfort, and disharmony. Stuffy rooms cause sleepiness. Rooms that are too cold or too hot make people uncomfortable. Windows bring cheer and openness to a room, although a distracting view reduces the group's productivity. Be aware of noise that interferes with the group's work, and try to control it as much as possible. It is better to stop the meeting and take time to reduce the noise than to try to carry on over the distraction.

Getting Involvement Early

The earliest stages of a meeting affect the level of participation later. Find an introductory activity that involves everyone during the first few minutes to let people know you really do want to hear from everyone. Make people feel involved right from the start. A few suggestions follow.

When people do not know one another, begin by having each person introduce himself or herself. List on a flip chart a few things you would like each person to tell the group—anything that may help people work better together. Examples are

- Name
- Current position
- Prior career or job
- Other team experience
- Expectations and hopes for this team
- Reasons for choosing this team
- Pet peeve about teams
- Favorite vacation spot
- A favorite food

Including something personal helps people relax, become better acquainted, and find things they have in common.

When holding the first meeting of a newly formed team or when starting a session that will emphasize teamwork, ask people to recall their first team experiences. After giving people some time to think, have each person tell the group

- What type of team it was
- When and where he or she was on the team
- What his or her role on the team was
- Positive or negative memories of being on the team
- What he or she learned about teams and being a team member from that experience

While people are speaking about their team experiences, record some of the ideas. Here are some thoughts about teams that might be aired:

- "The team was close-knit."
- "We accomplished a lot."
- "It was hard work."
- "We had fun!"
- "We were somewhat autonomous."
- "Our leader was demanding but fair."
- "Other work suffered."
- "We had enthusiasm and energy."

Later, summarize what the group said, emphasizing any points you wish to make about what makes a good team.

If you are working with a team whose members have been together for a while, ask each person to say a few words about what has happened since the last meeting that might affect the team's work. Jot down key points on a flip chart. Save this information and incorporate it into the meeting. If one or more people missed the last meeting, ask those who were present to suggest five words that describe that meeting. Write each word on a sheet of flip-chart paper. Then have someone tell the absentees why those words were used to describe the meeting and to summarize what went on at the last meeting. Ask the rest of the group members whether they have anything to add or change. Use their remarks to lead into your objective for the day. This activity starts everyone thinking about the last meeting, relaxes the group (and may even get a few laughs), brings the absentees up to date, and kicks off the current meeting.

The reason for undertaking an involvement activity at the beginning of the meeting is to balance participation right away and to establish the norm that everyone will be included. Daniels (1986, p. 16) said it this way: "Whatever is done during the first five minutes of a meeting establishes the norm state. . . . Providing an inclusion activity is the easiest and best way to deliberately shape the norm state into one of equal influence." The goal is to give everyone a chance to influence the outcome of the meeting. Meetings that begin with a long-winded presentation quickly lose participants' attention and make it less likely that they will become involved.

Summary

Using effective verbal techniques, such as asking open-ended questions, redirecting questions, and paraphrasing for clarity, keeps team members participating and keeps discussions focused and productive. Nonverbal techniques, such as silence, tone of voice, facial expressions, and movement in the room, are all important for setting a tone of productive participation and trust. Facilitators must pay attention as well to the meeting room environment and, when possible, set the room up for maximum interaction among meeting participants. In addition to the techniques listed above, effective facilitators direct the flow of a meeting so that everyone gets involved early on. Using these techniques gives participants ample encouragement to speak up and creates an atmosphere of trust and openness in a meeting.

12

Recording People's Ideas

In traditionally run meetings, a secretary records the meeting minutes, and they are read or distributed at a later date. Recording ideas in a participative meeting takes a different form and has a different purpose. A flip chart, displayed on an easel, is the most common medium used for recording ideas. The completed sheets become the working papers of a group in action. They contain ideas, data, opinions, alternatives, pros and cons, and issues that group members must consult as the meeting proceeds. When the group reaches consensus, the decision is written down for all to see and agree on. Action items, time frames, and responsible parties are published then and there.

The Power and Purpose of Recording Ideas

Possibly the most powerful argument for recording people's ideas is that it gives everyone an equal chance to influence and participate. Recording a person's idea for all to see acknowledges its value. The person who has thus contributed can then relax and listen to what others say or can think about others' contributions. The recorded idea is separated from the originator and later can be evaluated more objectively on its own merits.

Recording people's contributions also allows recall of those ideas. Recorded ideas are the team's notes; they become the group's memory, a data bank for reference as the meeting proceeds. When a meeting is in progress, many thoughts and ideas are put forth. People become overwhelmed and confused, and each one ends up remembering mostly what he or she considers important. When concentrating on their own ideas and how to express them, people do not hear or remember what others say. Or they may remember only part of a point. But when the ideas are posted around the room, people are free to refer to what has already been said.

Most people remember only a small percentage of what they hear (some say as little as 20 percent). We remember a much larger portion of what we both hear and see. Recording meeting data and decisions is therefore critical if a team is to be productive.

The information that is recorded also serves as a record of the group's progress. It is sometimes difficult to know where the group is on a topic or task. Referring to information on a flip chart can bring the group back from a tangent and keep everyone focused.

Keeping people from repeating the same things over and over again saves time too. The facilitator can discourage someone from bringing up a pet peeve repeatedly: "We have recorded that idea already" or "Is that the same as what Al said earlier?" When the group as a whole keeps covering the same territory again and again, the facilitator can move people on by saying, "Yes, that's a point we've written down. Let's move on to. . . ."

Why Use Flip Charts?

Even if you are dead set against using flip charts, please read on and at least circle the things that make sense to you. Then, if you are still determined not to use flip charts, try to find another way to accomplish what flip charts do so well. You may wish to start using them on a limited basis until you feel comfortable with them.

A flip chart is one of the facilitator's most valuable tools. It serves as a physical focus for the group, a place to direct everyone's attention and energy. Completed sheets from flip charts are the group's common notes, and as such they draw team members together in a combined, synergistic effort. Transparencies do not work as well, because the group can view only one at a time. If you must use transparencies, however, stop every half-hour or so and have them copied so that everyone has a working copy. This method creates a problem that does not exist with flip charts: everyone focuses on his or her own copy and the cohesiveness generated by using a common set of notes is lost.

Problem

Flip charts do create problems, however, that must be taken into account when planning a meeting. Here are some of the problems that people have pointed out:

- Using them may go against company culture.
- They are cumbersome and require extra effort to set up and use (a flip chart works best when it is set up on an easel, and easels are heavy and unwieldy).
- The individual sheets are difficult to tear off and post (masking tape must be available for posting).
- "I can't write legibly or large enough."
- The felt-tipped markers may dry up.
- "I can't listen, pay attention, and write all at the same time and a flip chart forces me to turn my back to people."
- Flip-chart sheets are difficult to copy, store, and reuse.

Potential flip chart problems

With all these disadvantages, why bother with flip charts? Flip charts are a highly effective means for quickly recording and posting people's ideas for immediate use in a meeting. They can be moved around in a room, labeled for all to see, and organized and used at a subsequent meeting, if necessary. The only thing that comes close to having the same advantages as flip charts are electronic white boards that allow information to be printed from them. These can be useful and provide many of the same advantages as flip charts. The drawbacks to these electronic white boards are that (1) they are expensive and, therefore, few meeting rooms have them; (2) once information is printed out for meeting members, people tend to focus downward on their own sheets of paper and not on a central place in the room; and (3) once the white board is erased, it isn't possible to go back to that information and edit or alter it. It either must be rewritten or everyone must alter his or her own sheets.

Although flip charts are effective, if they are not available meeting leaders should not give up on facilitating. Other methods can substitute for flip charts when necessary.

The Role of the Recorder

Either the facilitator or someone else may actually do the writing on flip charts. Many fine facilitators prefer to do their own recording. However, a facilitator who has trouble writing on a flip chart or summarizing people's comments should probably ask someone else to serve as recorder. The position of recorder can also be rotated so that everyone has a chance to participate in the meeting.

Whoever does the recording must be able to accurately capture people's ideas. He or she must listen carefully for the meaning of each idea and be careful not to leave out any ideas. If an idea closely resembles one that has already been recorded, the recorder can ask the participant if his or her comment is the same as the previous one. If the two ideas differ at all, even slightly, they should be recorded separately.

To remain neutral, the recorder must avoid jumping in with his or her own opinions or ideas. Participants will be annoyed if the recorder uses this central position to editorialize, add personal touches, or disagree with ideas being presented.

When someone else serves as the recorder, the facilitator needs to make sure that all inputs are being accurately represented. Sometimes it is up to the facilitator to slow down the comments so the recorder has time to capture them or to coach the recorder on the wording of an idea.

How to Record Ideas

The most difficult part of recording is to capture an idea accurately in a brief phrase. The challenge is to record a key word or phrase while using the participant's wording as much as possible. At times you may have to ask the participant to restate the idea in a few words. Taking too much liberty in paraphrasing may change the meaning. Thus it is better to select a few words used by the participant than to reword what was said.

While a participant is talking, listen attentively to everything, looking for a key phrase that will summarize the statement. Give people time to ramble a bit, to wrestle with their thoughts. Seldom do people come forth with brief, well-stated ideas when difficult subjects are being discussed. Also, if you try to write everything, you will run out of paper, markers, time, and stamina. When you think you have singled out the main idea, write what you think best captures the thought. If you are not certain you have phrased the idea correctly, check with the speaker: "Does this capture what you said?" Sometimes you will not be able to capture the main idea because the speaker is unclear, rambles, or states several ideas at once. Say something like "Can you summarize your idea in a phrase or two so I can record it here?"

Organizing the Ideas

A participative meeting can produce a lot of data. Several flip-chart sheets may be filled while group members discuss a question or brainstorm. Organizing the ideas that are recorded helps make them more accessible and useful.

To organize the ideas, you might first mark the beginning of each new one with a dash, a star, or a "bullet" (a large dot preceding an item). You could also number or letter each idea, especially if you think you will want to refer to them several times or categorize them for further consideration. For example, in a brainstorming session about purchasing new software, the following ideas might come up:

1. Replace the old software with Microsoft Word 6.0.1

2. Use both the old and the new software for a time and then evaluate

3. Test Word 6.0.1 by having 25 percent of the department use it first

4. List our current and future needs and then evaluate both pieces of software

Later, when the group is evaluating the ideas, each idea can be referred to by its number.

Some facilitators like to use two colors of felt-tipped markers. One color is used for the question, another for responses. Or colors are alternated as ideas are recorded, so people can more easily determine where one idea leaves off and another begins. Some facilitators write all the ideas in one color and use a second color to circle or underline key words when the ideas are being discussed or evaluated.

During a lengthy meeting, changing colors for each new portion of the meeting may help later, when the group is reviewing its work, reaching consensus, or planning follow-up. Changing colors is not necessary in this situation, however; the facilitator or recorder can number each chart as the meeting proceeds and post the charts in order throughout the meeting. Numbering the charts also helps later if the data are transcribed.

Creating and Writing on Flip Charts

Two excellent resources for someone who wants to use flip charts effectively are Brandt's (1986) *Flip Charts: How to Draw Them and How to Use Them* and Burn's (1996) *Flip Chart Power*. In his informative and well-illustrated book, Brandt explains how to lay out flip-chart posters, how to print them, and how to choose effective color combinations. His samples illustrate how effective simple graphics can be. In her book, Burn discusses and illustrates twenty-six uses for flip charts in meetings.

When using a flip chart during a meeting, you will find that your sheets are messier than those prepared ahead of time. However, some general principles apply to creating sheets, regardless of whether the sheets are prepared ahead of time or during the meeting.

First, write large and legibly so everyone can read what you have written. It is usually best to print, using either all capital letters or a combination of capital and lowercase letters. Select one handwriting style and stay with it, preferably the style in which you can write most quickly and legibly. Try to keep the size of your letters consistent.

Because you need to write quite a bit larger than you normally do, use your whole arm when you write. If you move only your wrist, as you do when writing at a desk, the letters will be too small. The larger the letter you want, the larger your arm movement should be. To make your letters bold and thick, hold the marker so the wide part of the tip touches the paper most of the time.

Even if your handwriting is poor, do not avoid using flip charts. A meeting record in poor handwriting is much better than no record at all. The goal is to have useful, not beautiful, sheets. For the same reason, write as quickly as you can. If you take too much time to write, you will defeat your larger purpose. A participative meeting should not drag on too long or people will lose their motivation to participate.

Most people worry about their spelling when they write on a flip chart. Even some of the best spellers have trouble in this situation, probably because the writing is large and they are pressured to write quickly and in front of others. There are several ways to handle poor spelling. One is to simply spell your best and expect a few misspelled words. Another is to state up front that you do not always spell well. Ask for help when you write a problem word. A third way (especially if you misspell words frequently) is to have someone who is a better speller record for you.

A second principle when using flip charts is to enhance your work with color or simple graphics whenever possible. Select colors that will make the pages useful and easy to read. The best colors for the main text are black, dark blue, and green, which show up the best from a distance. However, dark purple is also a readable color. Use red, orange, yellow, and other lighter colors for highlighting only. You can use a second color to write a few key words so they will stand out, to underline key phrases or words, to make "bullets," or to make the title stand out. A caution: Avoid using more than three colors on a page. Brandt (1986, p. 40) has this suggestion: "Two colors are better than one. Three aren't bad if done carefully and with purpose. More than three tend to be a bit much. The audience may have difficulty picking up accents or emphasis."

A graphic or picture always gets attention. Use graphics, however, not only to get attention but also for a purpose: to enhance, augment, or explain. Again, Brandt's book has a wealth of ideas for graphics, or use your own. Look through books on your topic or find art or children's books with simple pictures.

The third consideration when writing on flip charts is spacing. As a general rule, write only seven to twelve lines on a sheet prepared in advance. For a sheet with a few key phrases that you will refer to again and again, five or six lines is better. When recording people's ideas during a meeting, however, you need to get more lines on a sheet or you will use too many sheets and run out of room to post the ideas on walls. Some flip charts come with light blue grid lines spaced an inch apart. Write letters an inch high and skip an inch between lines, so that you have room for twelve to fifteen lines of writing per page.

The fourth principle is to post sheets during the meeting so they will be useful to the group. Some rooms do not have enough wall space or have walls that masking tape does not stick to. Masking tape is best for hanging sheets, unless your meeting room has strips of cork that you can push pins into. Transparent tape damages paint and wallpaper.

Handling and Storing Flip-Chart Pages

The quickest and most efficient way to post pages from a flip chart is to tear off small strips of inch-wide masking tape ahead of time and attach them to the easel that supports and displays the flip chart (see Figure 12.1). When you are ready to post a sheet, attach a piece of tape to the upper-left and upper-right sides of the paper before tearing the sheet off the flip chart. (Once the sheet has been torn off, you will have a hard time grabbing the tape, attaching it to the paper, and posting the sheet.) If you are short, ask someone who is taller to help you with posting.

FIGURE 12.1. Preparing Flip-Chart Pages for Posting.

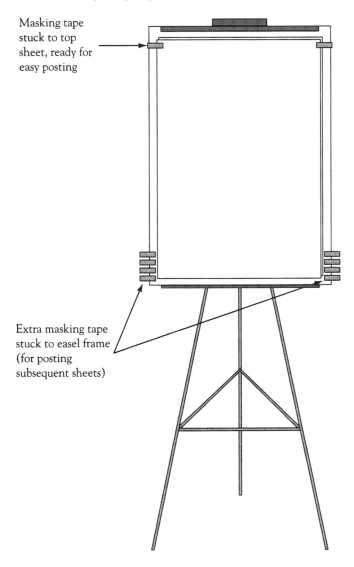

Masking tape
stuck to top
sheet, ready for
easy posting

Extra masking tape
stuck to easel frame
(for posting
subsequent sheets)

Tearing the sheets off the flip-chart pad can be a problem. Some paper just does not tear well. On the other hand, some paper has perforated holes, and some easels allow for better tearing than others. One way to tear off a sheet is to hold down the pad with one hand firmly at the top (the left if you are right-handed, vice versa if you are left-handed) and grasp the sheet at the bottom with the other hand. Then pull down on the sheet, starting the tear at the perforations. The sheet will usually tear easily then. This method is similar to how you would tear a piece of paper off an ordinary writing pad.

If this does not work, use the "confidence method," which not only always works but will give you a sense of power. The number-one rule here is to approach the flip chart with confidence. Grasp the sheet at the bottom left corner with your right hand (if you are right-handed). Lift it up, gathering momentum as you go. Grab the top of the easel with your left hand, and rip the sheet off the pad with one smooth tearing motion. Your right hand will make a large arc to the right. The edges of the paper will be a bit uneven, but the rest of the chart will be intact.

Other ways of tearing off sheets have been discovered, and each person will find a way that works best for him or her. The only reason the subject is discussed here is to let you know that people often have trouble tearing sheets off flip charts, that continually ripping up the hard work of the group can be frustrating (and funny), and that with a little practice tearing can be easy and natural.

Filled sheets sometimes need to be stored for later transcription or for reuse at another meeting. Arrange the sheets in chronological order and number them. If possible, store them flat. If not, roll them up and secure them with a rubber band. Label the roll on the outside so the charts can be found easily. You may want to roll them so the printed pages face up; in this way, when they are opened at a later date, they will not roll upward and cover up the wording.

Flip-Chart Pages as a Meeting Record

If the filled sheets are being transcribed as a meeting record, have the transcriber copy the exact wording and order of the sheets. People can recall the work of the meeting better if the sheets are not reorganized, cleaned up, and reworded. Editing the sheets may cause a group to struggle for quite some time to recapture what it did.

Summary

Flip-chart pages of information are an important part of the team's work. They serve as a working document during the meeting and an important record of the group's work and decisions, which can be transcribed or left as is for future reference.

13

Managing Group Process

Productive meetings require adequate time for participation, with enough structure to keep them on track and on schedule. Participation alone is not necessarily productive. Meetings that go on much longer than planned or that veer off the targeted schedule tend to be unproductive. Participants begin to fidget, wondering when the meeting will adjourn or when it will move on. Even highly interactive meetings need limits on time and topics to avoid wasting valuable time and energy on unrelated issues.

Stucture Without Strangulation

The facilitator's role is to balance open participation with structure. When the group strays too far, refer to the objectives of the meeting. Say something like "This subject is interesting and certainly important, but it isn't getting us any closer to our objective for today. Let's go back to. . . ." If the group members forget the process, remind them of what they are supposed to be doing: "Remember, we're just brainstorming now. We'll evaluate and discuss each idea later." It is also appropriate to ask a speaker how his or her point relates to the issue or objective: "Will you explain to us how your point relates to. . . ?" or "The points you're making are important, but they're not helping us accomplish our objective."

Although structure is important, it is a good idea to avoid too tight a structure. People need time to think, discuss, wander off the topic a little, and be creative. A certain amount of wandering can be productive. Side issues that relate to the main issue can be touched on. People can "vent" frustrations, and the facilitator can acknowledge the validity of those frustrations. These little "side trips" often bring out important data, giving the facilitator insights into people's perspectives and related concerns. These wanderings, however, should not dominate the meeting.

Summarizing and Bridging

From time to time, the facilitator should stop and *summarize* what has been said to refocus the group on its objective. Completed flip-chart sheets are a good tool for summarizing. Look back at the sheets with the group and highlight what has occurred so far. Say something like "We've heard a lot of good thoughts. Let me see whether I can summarize where we are now" or "We're getting away from our objective. Let's summarize and move on."

Let someone in the group summarize whenever possible: "Where are we at this point? Will someone please summarize what we have said so far?" The group then has the opportunity to reflect on both the content and the process of the meeting. But be prepared to summarize when someone else cannot. Some facilitators take a few notes during the discussion to help them summarize later.

After summarizing, move on to the next question or activity. Do not allow people to begin discussing ground that has already been covered, unless the group insists on doing so. You may be able to "read" the group and determine that moving on would be counterproductive. You must then come up with a process that will allow the group to complete its work on the old subject. One technique is to say, "We seem to need to discuss this some more. What is it we haven't covered?" Perhaps a topic needs to be dealt with separately, at another meeting. If so, record the topic on a flip chart and make it one of the action items for the next meeting. If the topic needs to be addressed before moving on, take time to discuss it fully and reach some kind of consensus. Otherwise, it may come up again and again throughout the meeting.

Another way to keep the group on track is to *bridge* from one activity or topic to another. Bridging consists of first summarizing the previous work and then explaining to the group what is going to happen next and how it relates to the previous work and to the meeting objective. For example: "We've listed several possible causes of the problem. Now let's take a different look at the problem by listing who and what could be benefiting from it." (The facilitator then begins a flip-chart sheet with the heading "Who/What May Be Benefiting from the Problem.") Another sort of bridge is a short break before the next activity.

Bridging can take place during a discussion as well. Point out how one person's comment relates to another's to provide a kind of "glue" holding together a lot of different points: "I think that supports what Brenna said earlier" or "Does that address one of your earlier concerns, Juan?"

Mirroring

A technique called *mirroring* allows the facilitator to help the group monitor itself. From time to time, the facilitator comments on either the content or the process of the meeting and then asks the group to respond. For example, the facilitator may mention that the group is commenting only on the disadvantages of a particular alternative. This observation then focuses the group on the *content* of its work. Or the facilitator might observe that, whenever someone brings up a radically different viewpoint, the rest of the group ignores that person. This observation focuses the group members on how they are working together, the process of the meeting. The facilitator may also mirror a ground rule that the group is violating: "Even though we agreed to hear everyone out, there's a lot of interrupting going on. How does this affect the team?" A comment like this encourages the group to adhere to its own norms and to change behaviors when those norms are violated.

Another way to mirror is to ask team members to comment on how the team is progressing, how well it is functioning, or how well it has met its objectives and expectations. The facilitator can ask for volunteers to comment or can ask each person separately to ensure that everyone is heard from. Encouraging team members to evaluate the team's progress from time to time fosters teamwork. It reinforces the idea that everyone has responsibility for the work of the team and that everyone's comments are worth listening to.

When the Group Is Stuck

Groups frequently get bogged down, become confused, or have trouble letting go of an issue. The facilitator can use several techniques to move a group forward when it gets stuck. If the group gets bogged down in specifics, move on to generalities: "We seem to be stuck on detail. Can someone give us the 'big picture' of what we're talking about?" When the group members are stuck on generalities, move them to specifics: "I'm hearing a lot of generalities; can someone give us some specifics?"

The group may be stuck on an issue that does not relate directly to the objectives. If this happens, tell the group you would like to stop for a few minutes and record the key points of this issue on a flip chart. Mention that this may be something the group will decide to work on at another time. Then ask the group to come back to the objectives and issue at hand.

One maxim that holds true for meetings and group work is "If people can get confused, they will." Their confusion is not necessarily a negative or bad thing—just a fact. Words can be interpreted differently. People have different perspectives, and any topic generally offers more information than people can deal with at one time. One of the facilitator's responsibilities, then, is to recognize confusion and help the group through it. Meetings can also be designed to minimize typical sources of confusion.

How should confusion be handled? First, acknowledge it. When appropriate, gently but firmly state that the group seems to be confused and that it needs to take time out to clear up the confusion. Second, mirror to the group what you are hearing. Third, try to sort out what the group is confused about. Use a flip chart to draw a model or number and list the confusing points; do whatever you can to explain the confusion. Check with the group members to see whether you have understood the problem. They may understand it better than you do. Then ask, "What can we do to clear this up and move on?" Or suggest a process that will help the group move on. For example, you may suggest saving some parts of the discussion for later in the process. You may refer to the topic that the confusion is about and clarify what was decided earlier. You may need to write something out for the whole group to see and then check to see whether everyone agrees on it. The solution depends, of course, on the situation. The key is to recognize and clear up the confusion so the group can proceed.

Using Subgroups to Get Things Done

Research has shown that the most productive group consists of five to nine members and that an odd number of people is better than an even number. With an odd number, tie votes and splits down the middle can be avoided. A facilitator with a group of more than nine people should consider breaking it down into smaller units from time to time to accomplish specific tasks.

Here are some circumstances that lend themselves to breaking a group into smaller units:

- When the task requires special expertise and not all members have that expertise

- When there is too much work and dividing the work will increase efficiency

- When you want to encourage certain people to work together—for example, to discourage cliques, to put together people who are highly motivated to work together, to give everyone a chance to work closely with everyone else, to allow one person's expertise to complement others', to have a more experienced or skilled person coach others

- When you want to give people a chance to choose which part of a project they want to work on

- When you want different groups to work on the same task, perhaps to foster more creativity, to generate several viable alternatives, or to increase everyone's learning and involvement

Whenever possible, let people form their own subgroups. Make certain each subgroup clearly understands its particular objective.

Even if you use subgroups, you should keep the larger group intact for some of the work. In particular, bring the subgroups back together frequently for discussion, review, and final decisions. If you do not, you may end up with several smaller teams instead of one large team.

"Reading" the Group and Making Adjustments

The facilitator's ability to read the group accurately is a critical and invaluable skill. Meetings generally do not run smoothly. Even with careful planning, people may be sidetracked to a more volatile issue or the process may not go very well. Facilitators must be able to recognize these problems and adjust. A productive meeting is not always a highly controlled one. The more participation there is, the more difficult it is to predict people's needs and responses—and the more difficult it is to conduct a meeting exactly as planned.

Reading the group during a meeting requires attentiveness to what is going on for individuals as well as for the group as a whole. A skilled facilitator pays attention to both the verbal and nonverbal behaviors of the participants. People signal their feelings through eye contact, posture, voice tone and volume, and facial expression. Their nonverbal clues may indicate

- Enthusiasm and high energy level
- Inattention (doing other things)
- Boredom or discomfort (yawning, looking away, reading)
- Confusion
- Anger, disdain, exasperation, and so on (rolling the eyes)
- Nervousness
- Agreement or satisfaction (nodding and smiling)

Verbal behaviors also offer important clues. Observe who is participating and how much. What is the conversation centering on? What is not being talked about? Is there a balance between facts and feelings? Is there general clarity or confusion? Is the leader in the background or foreground? Is leadership being shared among the group, or is one person clearly the leader? Are individual members hindering or helping the group's progress?

If most of the group members seem interested and involved, the meeting is probably going well. Some healthy disagreement usually means people are being open about their thoughts and feelings. However, a low energy level, apathy, or boredom may indicate that the group needs a change of pace. You can revitalize the group with a short break, a new activity, a different process, a change to subgroups, a new topic, or even adjournment and continuation of the meeting at a later time.

Frequently you will know that something is wrong but not know what it is. When this happens, ask the group, "What's happening right now for people?" or "We've lost much of our energy; what do we need to do now?" When the group has too much energy and is becoming unruly, you might say, "There's a lot of energy on this topic, but we're losing our productivity. Let's discuss one point at a time."

Sometimes groups focus too much on either the facts or the feelings connected with a topic. When this happens, try suggesting that the group think about the topic from another angle. For example, if the group is expressing a lot of strong feelings without many facts, intervene and say, "We've aired a lot of feelings on this issue, and this is good. Let's bring out some of the facts." If the group is putting forth facts but avoiding the feelings associated with an issue, steer the group by saying, "We've covered many facts related to this issue. What are some of your feelings about what we are discussing?"

An imbalance of participation is another problem. You can restore balance by seeking the opinions of quieter individuals: "Kevin, we haven't heard from you on this issue. What are some of your thoughts?" If one side of the room is quieter than the other or one subgroup is not participating, ask for some input from that group: "I'd like to hear from. . . ."

Just remember that the facilitator's role is to guide the process, leading the group so that it accomplishes its work. If the meeting process has to be adjusted to make this happen, then the facilitator must either make adjustments or accept the suggestions of meeting participants, who sometimes have better ideas about what will work. The facilitator is not divine; he or she cannot lay out a perfect meeting each time. It is more likely that the facilitator will have to navigate the meeting, making adjustments to make participation productive.

Handling Difficult Individuals

From time to time, any member of a group may become difficult. A well-focused and well-facilitated meeting can overcome most difficult situations, but there will always be some.

Facilitators can follow some general rules when a difficult situation arises. First, handle the problem before it gets out of hand. Second, do not embarrass people, because "embarrassed kittens become tigers." Third, protect everyone's self-esteem throughout any difficult situation. And fourth, take control in a firm, positive, constructive way.

How do you know when to intervene? A good rule of thumb is to ask yourself whether the group's productivity and enjoyment are being affected. If the answer is "yes," then it is time to do something.

When someone is hurting the productivity of the group, you have three choices: to deal with this person in front of the group, to deal with the issue during a break, or to ignore the problem. For the sake of productivity, the last choice is probably not a good one. Sometimes the problem goes away without any intervention, but if it does not, the facilitator will eventually need to do something.

When you can constructively and positively handle the situation in front of the group, do so to maintain productivity. Here are some suggestions:

- "Matt, you've made several fine points today. Now I would like to hear comments from someone else."

- "Kathy, you made that point earlier. See, it's recorded on the flip chart."

- "Jim, is there something you and Bill would like to share with the rest of the group?" or "Jim and Bill, I'd like to have only one meeting at a time." Move toward those engaged in the side conversation, and then wait until they stop.

- "Angela, it seems that you don't agree we should take this approach. Why? What would you like to see happen?" This technique gives the person a chance to vent feelings and gives others a chance to address the person's concerns.

- Ask a withdrawn, overly quiet person to help you.

If you cannot resolve the problem gracefully in front of the entire group, wait until break time to discuss the problem with the individual. You might want to speak to a perpetual latecomer at the break. Or if one group member has been vociferously opposing someone else's idea, you can say something like "Joe, you seem to take issue with Mary every time she addresses XYZ. After the break, would you be willing to give us some of your ideas about how you would rather proceed?"

Several types of people often create problems during meetings. The *overly talkative* person who comments too frequently is one of them. Others become discouraged or frustrated waiting for him or her to finish, and the group loses the benefit of other viewpoints. This person may be a show-off or a windbag. He or she may also be exceptionally well-informed and eager to contribute. Regardless, when this person dominates the meeting, the group's energy level will go down, and others will withdraw. Sometimes the group members will correct this type of person, but when they do not, the facilitator must intervene to maintain productivity. As the facilitator, you can cut across this person's talk with a summarizing statement and a direct question to someone else—for example: "That's an interesting point; now let's hear from Jennifer."

Another kind of person who poses a problem is the one who *rambles*—who talks about things other than the subject, uses far-fetched analogies, or gets lost before reaching the point. When a rambler stops for breath, thank him or her, refocus attention by restating the relevant points and reminding the group of its objective, and move on. You may indicate, "We need to get back to our subject."

Other people may be *inarticulate*. They have contributions to make but lack the ability to put those contributions into the proper words. You can help out by listening and then restating the person's ideas: "Let me restate that." Help such a person express his or her ideas so that they make sense to the group.

A different problem occurs when someone just will *not talk*. Try to determine what is motivating the person, whether boredom, indifference, timidity, or feelings of superiority or insecurity. Is the person new to the group or from a culture that believes it is rude to jump in or interrupt someone else? Your action will depend on the person's motivation. Seek suitable ways to involve the person. Ask direct questions that you are sure the person can answer. Ask for his or her agreement or opinion on views expressed by others.

When someone is definitely wrong and continues to come up with obviously *incorrect comments*, the group will become annoyed. Wrong information also gets in the way of productivity. This situation must be handled delicately. As a facilitator, you can intervene with "I can see how you feel," "That's one way of looking at it," or "I see your point, but can we reconcile that with the true situation?" An even more direct approach would be to ask "What are some facts to support what you are saying?"

The *obstinate* individual is one who just will not budge. He or she does not see the point and will not go along with the rest of the group. Try to get the others to help this person see their point of view. When you are ready to move on, say something like "I'm sure you have a reason for your point of view, but I'd like you to try to consider the group's viewpoint for now."

The *latecomer* is perpetually late to group meetings or darts in and out of meetings to carry on other business. Avoid confronting the person in front of the group. Wait until during a break or after the meeting. Find out why the person is always late (there may be an important reason). Point out why this behavior is disruptive, and ask the latecomer to help you figure out a solution. When the latecomer arrives, ask someone else to quickly review what is going on, and then continue.

Similar to the latecomer is the *early leaver*. A person who leaves before the meeting ends drains the energy of the group and misses the most important part of the meeting, which is reaching consensus and closure. At the beginning of the meeting, check to see whether everyone can stay until the end. If all participants commit to staying until the end of the meeting, a potential early leaver is less likely to sneak out. If you do not need everyone until the end, tell the group ahead of time. Also, check to see that your meetings keep to the scheduled time, are not too unstructured or boring, and involve everyone in the group.

Summary

There are a number of skills facilitators can employ to manage the complex nature of team meetings.

A good facilitator provides structure without forcing the process and is alert to team members' verbal and nonverbal cues during the meeting. Watching the group for signals, a facilitator judges when to move the group ahead and when to let it go. A facilitator learns when to summarize and bridge to the next activity, when to check with the group as to what it wants to do, and when to stop the group and intervene when a particular method is not working. Keeping tuned in to what is going on in the team meeting helps a facilitator guide the process so that the team can get its best work done.

14

Reaching Consensus and Closure

Consensus is a point of maximum agreement so action can follow. According to Doyle and Straus (1976), it is a win-win solution, in which "everyone feels that he or she has won. . . . a solution that does not compromise any strong convictions or needs" (p. 56). Consensus is not achieved by voting, by imposing a win-lose outcome, by dictating the conclusion, or by people's abdicating or giving in. To reach consensus, group members share ideas, discuss and evaluate, debate, organize and prioritize ideas, and struggle to reach the best conclusion together. Reaching consensus is the act of gaining general agreement. A good test for consensus is to ask the question, "Can you support this decision?" If everyone can support it, the group has achieved 100 percent consensus.

When to Use Consensus

Consensus is not always the best strategy. In some cases, reaching consensus does not result in a better decision or outcome. Group members are capable of unanimously agreeing on a completely incorrect solution to a problem. On certain occasions, however, consensus remains a highly desirable goal. When a group must make an important decision that requires the commitment of all members, consensus is the best approach.

The process of reaching a consensus takes time and should not be rushed. The process works best when it has been carefully planned, when the instructions are clear, and when the facilitator is skilled in using such objective techniques as brainstorming and prioritization processes. Studies have shown that groups using a systematic, rational method to make decisions and solve problems make higher quality decisions than do groups that do not proceed rationally. The facilitator plays a critical role in seeing that the group uses a rational method and a structured process (Collins and Guetzkow, 1964).

Because it takes time and skill, consensus should be reserved for important decisions requiring a high degree of support and commitment from those who will implement the decisions.

How to Make Consensus Work

To make consensus work, the leader must become skilled at separating the content of the team's work (the task itself) from the process (how the team goes about doing the task). But the process is what requires the most attention.

One of the facilitative leader's key responsibilities is to help others solve their own problems. The leader who wants his or her team members to become skilled at problem solving will teach them a process for solving problems, without solving the problems for them.

The Problem-Solving Process

The problem-solving process involves the following steps, each of which requires group participation:

1. Identify the problem or goal

2. Generate alternative solutions

3. Establish objective criteria

4. Decide on a solution that best fits the criteria

5. Proceed with the solution

6. Evaluate the solution

A meeting should be structured so that everyone knows exactly which step is being worked on at any point.

Discussion and creative thinking are more likely to occur when the steps are introduced with open questions, such as the following:

1. *Identify the Problem or Goal.* Problem: What is the problem? How do you see the problem? What seems to be causing the problem? If the problem were solved, what would happen? *Goal:* What are we trying to achieve? Where do we want to end up?

2. *Generate Alternative Solutions.* What are possible solutions? If we had no restraints, what would we do to solve the problem?

3. *Establish Objective Criteria.* What objective and measurable criteria must the solution meet?

4. *Decide on the Alternative That Best Fits the Criteria.* How well does each alternative meet our criteria? Which solution best fits the criteria? Is this the best decision?

5. *Implement the Decision.* Who needs to do what and by when?

6. *Evaluate the Solution.* How well did the solution solve the problem?

A skilled facilitator can use other group processes to help achieve consensus. Remember when using any of the following techniques to keep the L.E.A.D. model in mind. First, explain the purpose of each process to the group. Second, motivate group members to become meaningfully involved. Third, aim for—but do not rush—consensus. Allow time for meandering, disagreement, and discussion. Move the group members to consensus by asking, "Do we have general agreement on this point?" When the members do not agree, allow time for more discussion. At some point agreement may become necessary. You can move the group toward action by stating, "Even though we have differences of opinion on this point, we do agree on. . . . I suggest that now we move forward so we can achieve our objective."

Identifying the Problem

When people sense a problem, they are usually reacting to problem symptoms. Something is happening that should not be happening, or something should be happening, but is not. But such symptoms are side effects of the real problem, which usually lies beneath the surface. The leader's role is to guide the group in identifying the real problem or the various parts of the real problem (problems in organizations tend to be complex). Questioning and labeling are two techniques the leader can use to involve the group in problem identification.

Questioning. Much can be discovered about a problem and its root cause through the simple process of asking questions. The point is to understand the whole problem before rushing to solve what may be only a symptom of the problem. By answering questions, people gain a broader understanding of the problem and avoid jumping to premature conclusions.

Begin by asking these two questions: "What is happening that should not be?" and "What should be happening that is not?" Record each group member's input and then post the list. The next step is to involve the group in asking and answering a series of questions together. Use a flip-chart sheet on which you have printed the words "Who," "What," "When," and "Where." Ask the group to identify *who* is involved with the problem; *what* materials, processes, equipment, and so forth are involved with the problem; *when* the problem occurs; and *where* the problem occurs. Record each input as you go, and then ask the flip side of the who/what/when/where questions: "Who is *not* involved with the problem?" "What materials, processes, equipment, and so on are *not* involved with the problem?"

Here are some additional questions you can ask the group to answer:

(handwritten marginal note: or individuals separately)

- "How do you see what is going on?"
- "How does the problem affect you?"
- "What is likely to happen if the problem is not addressed and resolved?"
- "What are likely causes of the problem?"
- "What seems to be the real problem?"
- "What seems to be the root cause of the problem?"
- "What are the key benefits of solving the problem?"

Continue asking questions until you begin to hear the same answers over and over again. Then ask the group members whether they feel the need to gather more data before going on to the next step. If they do, assign responsibilities for gathering the data and plan to deal with the problem at the next meeting. But once the group has sufficient data, you can move on.

Labeling.   The next step is labeling the problem in such a way that the group can focus on its solution. You have two ways to do this. The first is to state the problem in terms of what needs to happen and what is preventing it from happening. Here are some examples:

- "Our goal is to handle customer assignments on time and in a quality way, but our customers continually clamor to get their work assigned number-one priority with a due date of 'as soon as possible.'"

- "Lack of communication among the specialists in our department makes it difficult to provide service to our customers when someone is absent from the office."

- "Budgets are due on October 1, but it is September 20 and we still do not have the volume projections for next year."

   The second way to label the problem is to state it in the form of a question:

- "How can we accomplish our goal of handling customer assignments on time and in a quality way when our customers continually clamor to get their work assigned number-one priority with a due date of 'as soon as possible'?"

- "How can we improve communication among the specialists in our department so that customers can receive service when someone is absent from the office?"

- "How can we receive the volume projections in time to get the budget in by October 1?"

Generating Alternatives

The most common way to generate alternatives is through brainstorming. After generating as many alternatives as possible with brainstorming, those ideas may be grouped into categories through the process of clustering. Later the clustered ideas can be dealt with in an organized manner.

Brainstorming. Most people are familiar with brainstorming, although few have experienced it in the way it works best. What is supposed to happen during a brainstorming session is that people think of as many ideas as possible—any idea is acceptable. The goal is to get as many ideas as possible to look at. Without a skilled facilitator, however, the brainstorming process frequently gets mixed up with the process of discussing and evaluating the ideas. People in the group say things like "That's an interesting idea. However, it won't work here because. . . ." or "Yes, but what about the policy that forbids. . . ?" This is not brainstorming in the classic sense.

If you allow the group to deviate from the correct process, you diminish the value of brainstorming. To facilitate a brainstorming session, you should begin by posting and reviewing with the group the following guidelines:

Guidelines for Brainstorming

- Strive for quantity, not quality. The more ideas, the better!
- Defer judgment of ideas, even your own.
- Let your mind go! Wild ideas are welcome and may lead to a breakthrough.
- Piggyback on others' ideas, or combine one or more ideas.
- Do not react to or discuss any ideas at this time.

Then make sure the group follows these steps in order:

1. Give people a problem or a question to focus on.

2. Have <u>each person write down privately</u> as many ideas as he or she can think of, no matter how far-fetched, that might solve the problem or answer the question. (Sometimes the most far-fetched ideas inspire the best solution.)

3. <u>Record and post all ide</u>as without discussing or evaluating them.

4. <u>Encourage people to build on one another's ideas</u> and continue recording and posting all ideas.

5. <u>Clarify the ideas</u>. Give everyone a chance to look at the ideas and ask questions about the meaning of any idea. Do not evaluate any of the ideas at this time.

The following paragraphs present a more detailed look at each of the five steps:

1. *Give people a problem or a question to focus on.* To start the brainstorming session, post the key question to be addressed for all the group to see. If you have labeled a problem in the form of a question, you can use the label to focus the group. For example: "How can we improve communication among the specialists in our department so that customers can receive service when someone is absent from the office?"

2. *Have each person write down privately as many ideas as he or she can think of, no matter how far-fetched, that might solve the problem or answer the question.* <u>It is important to allow time for people</u> to <u>think privately, because once the ideas begin to be posted,</u> indi<u>viduals may alter their own thinking</u>. Emphasize that "any idea goes," and encourage people not to edit or censor their own ideas.

3. *Record and post all ideas without discussing or evaluating them.* One approach that works well is to proceed around the room, person by person, and <u>solicit one idea from each person</u>. Complete

this process again and again until people have run out of ideas. Remember to capture the ideas accurately and to write down all new contributions. Tear off the filled flip-chart sheets and post them for all to see. If someone's idea sounds like one that has already been recorded, ask that person if his or her idea is the same. If so, do not record it again. If the person says it is different, post the idea. (When recording the ideas, you might want to number them; the numbers will help when you are referring to and grouping the ideas.) People will be tempted to ask for clarification or expansion of an idea or to comment on an idea. Disallow these types of comments, explaining that discussion and clarification will come later.

Watch for violations of the brainstorming guidelines and remind participants to keep to them, if necessary. Your role as a facilitator is to keep the ideas coming and record them as quickly as possible. Don't edit the ideas or change people's wording; just get the ideas down. Only after all ideas are recorded do you move on to clarification of the ideas.

4. *Encourage people to build on one another's ideas and continue recording and posting all ideas.* Ask whether anyone has any ideas that are new or that build on what someone else has suggested. Do not be surprised if you have several sheets filled with ideas at this point.

5. *Clarify the ideas.* After all ideas have been generated and recorded, give the group a chance to ask questions about them. The person who contributed the idea can be asked to comment on the intent or meaning of the idea. The group's goal is to clarify and understand each idea, not to evaluate it or discuss it in detail.

Clustering. Evaluating twenty to fifty ideas can be quite cumbersome. Clustering is grouping the ideas into categories to help organize the evaluation process. If only a few ideas are generated, this step is probably not necessary. However, brainstorming usually generates a long list of ideas, many of which relate to other ideas.

The first step in clustering is to ask the group which ideas are related. Use letters or different colored markers or stickers to indicate which ideas can be grouped together for ease of discussion. Ask for general agreement here. If some group members prefer to keep an idea separate, honor their reasoning and move on. Some ideas will not lend themselves to clustering.

The second step is to label each idea group with an appropriate title. For example, all ideas relating to improving human relations could be grouped together under "Human Relations." Ideas relating to monetary resources and budget could be called "Money" or "Budget." Make a list of the categories somewhere, and list either the ideas themselves or the numbers of the ideas that go into each category. If you adjourn the meeting and give someone the assignment of rewriting the ideas in clusters, caution him or her not to change any wording. No individual should be given the group's responsibility to weed out and refine the ideas.

Clustering does not mean that all the ideas in one cluster are going to be adopted or that all the ideas in another cluster will be thrown out. Nor does it mean that a category that contains numerous ideas is more important than a single idea that stands alone. Clustering simply helps people consider and discuss all the ideas in one category at a time. Ideas should still be considered separately, each for its own merit. If subteams are formed, each subteam can be assigned a category to review. If the entire team deals with all of the brainstormed ideas, clustering helps organize the discussion. Later, if you ask people to prioritize the ideas according to their value, be sure people consider the ideas separately, unless the entire team has agreed to group two or more ideas into one.

Establishing Criteria

The next step in the problem-solving process is to get people to agree on what criteria they are going to use to evaluate the alternatives. Some argue that criteria should be established before brainstorming. Obviously, the brainstorming step influences the criteria step and vice versa. However, if criteria are established after brainstorming, the brainstorming process can be more creative and unrestrained. Another advantage is that the brainstorming process is likely to open people's minds to new ideas and help keep them from being rigid in the criteria-setting process.

There are two types of criteria: (1) *essential* criteria that solutions *must* meet, and (2) *desirable* criteria that it would be nice to meet. Ask the group to classify the criteria as either essential or desirable.

Also make sure that each criterion is objective and measurable. Instead of specifying that something be affordable, for example, identify what "affordable" is. An essential criterion might be a solution that costs less than $100,000. Setting measurable criteria will ease the process of reaching consensus.

Evaluating Alternatives

Any alternatives that do not meet the essential criteria can be eliminated. Those that remain can be evaluated on how well they meet the desirable criteria.

Sometimes a worthy idea is eliminated because it does not fit the essential criteria. You may want to suggest that the group consider changing such an idea so that it meets the essential criteria.

One or more solutions may fit both the essential and desirable criteria. At this stage the group members must come to a consensus about which solution best fits the criteria. They may decide that more than one solution must be implemented to solve the problem.

Implementing the Decision

The next step is to break down the best alternative into manageable tasks, things that must be done to put the decision into effect. The question is "Who needs to do what and by when?"

First, have people in the group think of anything that must be done to implement the decision. Try to list things that can be done by one person, so that responsibilities can be assigned. Second, number all the tasks; then indicate beside each task which others must be completed before that particular task can be started. Third, estimate the amount of time it will take to complete each task. Last, plot the tasks on a chart with a time line to help the group implement its decision on schedule.

Evaluating the Solution

One of the most important things a leader-facilitator can do to develop a mature team is to help it to evaluate its own progress. When a problem has been solved and the solution has been implemented, have the team evaluate how well the solution solved the problem. What still needs to be addressed? Team members should also evaluate progress toward individual goals (the tasks), as well as their progress in working together. At first, the facilitator should build time for evaluation into the group meetings. Later, as the team matures, members will undoubtedly initiate their own evaluation.

Here are some questions to use in evaluating the results of a task and how well people worked together:

- "What went well as far as the task is concerned?"

- "What should we do differently next time as far as the task is concerned?"

- "What went well as far as the team's working together is concerned?"

- "How shall we work together differently next time?"

If the group is large, divide it into two subgroups. Have one subgroup answer the first two questions and the other subgroup answer the other two. Then have each subgroup report its findings to the rest of the team.

Keeping People on Track

When a group is involved in a problem-solving session, the facilitator is responsible for keeping the group members on track. To begin with, the facilitator must give clear directions about how to carry out each step. He or she will also need to steer people back to the topic when they wander. People's minds do not always work in an orderly fashion. For example, during the brainstorming process, people will naturally want to discuss the ideas as they are generated instead of waiting until later. Or when the group is establishing criteria, people are likely to begin discussing their advantages and disadvantages. In either case, the facilitator will have to intervene.

The group processes suggested here are only a few basic ones. The literature on group decision making, problem solving, and communication suggests many more techniques for bringing groups to consensus or helping them work together more productively (see the References and Bibliography). Some are more difficult to implement than others. Leader-facilitators must practice to find the ones they and their group are most comfortable with.

Reaching Closure

At several points in the problem-solving process, consensus must be reached before the next step begins. At each juncture, the facilitator should state what the group has agreed on and then check with the group to make sure the statement is accurate. The best way to make sure everyone has agreed to the same thing is to write out what was decided and post it for all to see. If action planning is part of the group's work, for example, list the actions that must be performed, those who will undertake the actions, and the deadlines for completing them.

Documenting agreements for all to see serves several purposes:

- Clarifies what people are agreeing to
- Provides a record of what was decided
- Motivates people to keep their agreements (their names appear publicly beside assignments)
- Brings absent members accurately up to date
- Focuses attention and energy on the actions that must be carried out

Other Useful Techniques

Other useful techniques for moving toward closure include prioritizing and four-box analysis.

Prioritizing

A group frequently has too many issues at hand, too many problems that need to be addressed, or too many goals to deal with all at once. When such is the case, prioritizing will help. The first step

is to compile a list of what needs to be addressed on a flip-chart
sheet and label each item in sequence with a letter of the alpha-
bet. Then open up a discussion by saying, "Which of these should
have the highest priority for our team now?" After group members
have had a chance to think about and discuss the question, ask
them to pick the three items (or four or five, whichever seems
appropriate) that they think deserve the highest priority. Ask each
member to write the letters of these items on a 3" × 5" index card
that you distribute.

To compile the results, you can have each person put one
mark on the sheet beside the items he or she chose or collect the
cards and tally the results during a break. Have the members work
as a group to pick the three to five items that received the most
votes. Then ask people to comment on their own selections. Once
the top items have been discussed, ask whether anyone wants to
change his or her vote. Once the final voting is finished, pick the
top three to five items and ask, "Can everyone support (name
the items) as our highest priority?" Write these items on a separate
sheet as a record of the group's decision.

An alternative is to have each person assign points to his or
her own top items. Give each person a total of ten points to distribute, with the most points for the highest priority choice and
the least points for the lowest priority choice. (The facilitator can
decide whether to allow people to assign zeroes.) Here are some
examples:

First person:	C	7 points
	F	2 points
	G	1 point
Second person:	A	2 points
	R	8 points
	M	0 points

Tally the points for each lettered item. The ones with the highest numbers of points are the highest priority items.

Four-Box Analysis

When a group is struggling through a difficult period, four-box analysis is a method it can use to regain direction and a sense of purpose. This technique allows the team members to deal with any aspect of their work together, to recognize strengths they may have been overlooking, and to pinpoint areas for improvement. The team must answer four questions:

1. What is not going well and is flexible (can change)?
2. What is not going well and is firm (not likely to change or not within the group's power to change)?
3. What is going well and is flexible (can change)?
4. What is going well and is firm (not likely to change or not within the group's power to change)?

Figure 14.1 shows how these questions structure a four-box diagram. Responses to question 1 are those things that present the greatest opportunities for change. They are not going well, yet there is the potential for change. Responses to question 2 are things that are not going well but are out of the group's control. They are things about which the group can do nothing, so spending time and energy on them is unproductive. Responses to question 3 are things that are going well but, because they could change, need to be maintained. The group should continue to pay attention to these things and not take them for granted. Responses to question 4 represent those things the group can count on. They are going well and are not likely to change. These are the group's assets.

FIGURE 14.1. Four-Box Analysis.

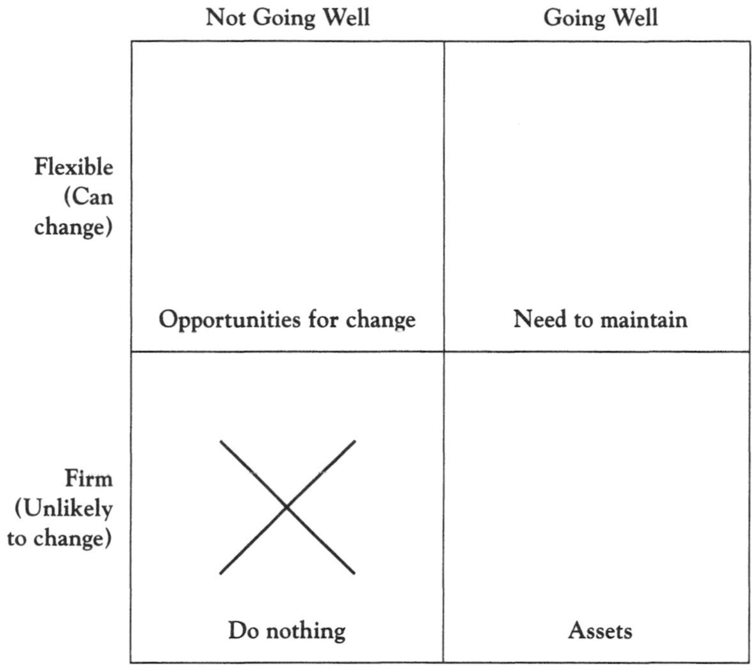

Once group members have collectively answered these questions and looked at their responses, they can focus on "opportunities for change." These are the things that need the attention of the group. The facilitator can suggest prioritizing them or using some other means to decide where to begin.

A group that has been struggling for some time should probably pick one thing to focus on at a time. It might also pick something that will be easy and quick to change, so it can feel successful right away. Starting with a difficult item may discourage the group even further.

The problem-solving process, brainstorming, prioritizing, and four-box analysis methods mentioned in this chapter are but a few of the many processes that facilitators can employ to manage group process successfully. The purpose of this book is to present basic concepts of facilitative leadership and the primary facilitation skills that support them, and it does not present a complete selection of tools. In the author's book, *The Facilitator Excellence Handbook* (Rees, 1998), there are several chapters devoted to methods and tools, as well as a discussion on how to design an effective facilitation. To help teams generate and organize material, a team leader can choose from such methods as structured rounds, T-charts, affinity diagramming, fishbone diagramming, flow charting, and matrix diagramming. To facilitate teams in ranking and evaluating material they have generated, a team leader has numerous approaches to choose from, including multi-voting, ranking and prioritizing, nominal group technique, force-field analysis, quadrant diagrams, and decision matrices. In the book mentioned above, each of these methods is presented, with instructions on how to facilitate them. Another helpful book, which includes some of the above methods as well as others, is *The Quality Toolbox* (Tague, 1995).

Follow-Up

Once team members agree on a plan of action, they must continue getting together to keep track of their progress. If too much time passes between meetings, team members may lose their motivation and deadlines may go by unnoticed.

Follow-up meetings do not have to be long. They can be a few minutes in length. But it is important for team members to come together to ensure that their decisions are being implemented and their problems are being solved. (They do not have to go through the whole process of decision making and problem solving again.) Without timely follow-up to the work that has been done, the team will be less motivated to work hard on the next problem.

And if no time is set aside for follow-up, a question arises: Should time have been spent on the problem in the first place?

This question brings us full circle. A meeting must have a clear objective, and that objective must be worth the time required not only for meeting but also for following up. Two of the most common errors that leaders make are (1) holding meetings without clear, published objectives and (2) failing to follow up on the work done at those meetings. Meetings are a waste of time if nothing valuable is accomplished or if the valuable work that is done goes nowhere.

Summary

A truly facilitative leader views meetings as a primary means of getting people to work together and puts time and effort into planning and leading meetings. The techniques and processes outlined in this book are only the basic tools for drawing successfully on team members' skills, knowledge, and diversity. The tools are not ends in themselves, nor are they exclusive or even unique to this book. But they will help leaders face the tremendous challenges of managing in an ever-changing, uncertain, and demanding world.

References and Bibliography

Bradford, D. L., and Cohen, A. R. (1984). *Managing for excellence*. New York: John Wiley & Sons.

Bradford, L. P. (1976). *Making meetings work: A guide for leaders and group members*. San Francisco, CA: Jossey-Bass/Pfeiffer.

Brandt, R. C. (1986). *Flip charts: How to draw them and how to use them*. San Francisco, CA: Jossey-Bass/Pfeiffer.

Burn, B. E. (1996). *Flip chart power: Secrets of the masters*. San Francisco, CA: Jossey-Bass/Pfeiffer.

Collins, B. E., and Guetzkow, H. (1964). *A social psychology of group processes for decision-making*. New York: John Wiley & Sons.

Daniels, W. R. (1986). *Group power 1: A manager's guide to using task-force meetings*. San Francisco, CA: Jossey-Bass/Pfeiffer.

Doyle, M., and Straus, D. (1976). *How to make meetings work*. New York: Jove.

Fisher, B. A. (1980). *Small group decision making* (2nd ed.). New York: McGraw-Hill.

Fisher, K., Rayner, S., Belgard, W., and the Belgard, Fisher, Rayner team. (1995). *Tips for teams*. New York: McGraw-Hill.

Glassman, E. (1991). *The creativity factor: Unlocking the potential of your team*. San Francisco, CA: Jossey-Bass/Pfeiffer.

Gordon, T. (1977). *Leader effectiveness training (L.E.T.): The no-lose way to release the productive potential of people*. Ridgefield, CT: Wyden.

Harrington-Mackin, D. (1996). *Keeping the team going*. New York: American Management Association.

Heider, J. (1985). *The tao of leadership*. New York: Bantam.

Howell, J. L. (1995). *Tools for facilitating team meetings*. Seattle, WA: Integrity Publishing.

Hunter, D., Bailey, A., and Taylor, B. (1992). *The zen of facilitation: The handbook for people meeting with a purpose*. Tucson, AZ: Fisher Books.

Hunter, D., Bailey, A., and Taylor, B. (1995). *The art of facilitation: How to create group synergy*. Tucson, AZ: Fisher Books.

Kaner, S. (1996). *Facilitator's guide to participatory decision-making*. Gabriola Island, BC: New Society Publishers.

Katzenbach, J. R., and Smith, D. K. (1993). *The wisdom of teams: Creating the high-performance organization*. New York: HarperCollins.

Kearny, L. (1995). *The facilitator's toolkit: Tools and techniques for generating ideas and making decisions in groups*. Amherst, MA: HRD Press.

Kinlaw, D. C. (1993). *Team-managed facilitation: Critical skills for developing self-sufficient teams*. San Francisco, CA: Jossey-Bass/Pfeiffer.

Montebello, A. R. (1994). *Work teams that work: Skills for managing across the organization*. Minneapolis, MN: Best Sellers Publishing.

Mosvick, R. K., and Nelson, R. B. (1987). *We've got to start meeting like this!* Glenview, IL: Scott, Foresman.

Peck, M. S. (1978). *The road less traveled*. New York: Simon & Schuster.

Pfeiffer, J. W., and Ballew, A. C. (1988). *Presentation and evaluation skills in human resource development*. San Francisco, CA: Jossey-Bass/Pfeiffer.

Pokras, S. (1989). *Systematic problem-solving and decision-making*. Los Altos, CA: Crisp.

Rees, F. (1991). *How to lead work teams: Facilitation skills*. San Francisco, CA: Jossey-Bass/Pfeiffer.

Rees, F. (1997). *Teamwork from start to finish: 10 steps to results*. San Francisco, CA: Jossey-Bass/Pfeiffer.

Rees, F. (1998). *The facilitator excellence handbook: Helping people work creatively and productively together*. San Francisco, CA: Jossey-Bass/Pfeiffer.

Saint, S., and Lawson, J. R. (1994). *Rules for reaching consensus*. San Francisco, CA: Jossey-Bass/Pfeiffer.

Sayles, L. R. (1990, Spring). Leadership for the nineties: Challenge and change. *Issues & Observations*, pp. 8–11.

Schindler-Rainman, E., and Lippitt, R. (1988). *Taking your meetings out of the doldrums* (rev. ed.). San Francisco, CA: Jossey-Bass/Pfeiffer.

Scholtes, P. R. (1988). *The team handbook*. Madison, WI: Joiner Associates.

Schrage, M. (1990). *Shared minds: The new technologies of collaboration*. New York: Random House.

Schwarz, R. M. (1994). *The skilled facilitator: Practical wisdom for developing effective groups*. San Francisco, CA: Jossey-Bass.

Silberman, M. (1999). *101 ways to make meetings active: Surefire ideas to engage your group*. San Francisco, CA: Jossey-Bass/Pfeiffer.

Tagliere, D. A. (1993). *How to meet, think and work to consensus*. San Francisco, CA: Jossey-Bass/Pfeiffer.

Tague, N. R. (1995). *The quality toolbox*. Milwaukee, WI: ASQC Quality Press.

About the Author

Fran Rees is a consultant, trainer, and author who lives in Chandler, Arizona. In the year 2001, her consulting firm, Rees & Associates, celebrates its fifteenth year in business. Since the publication of the first edition of *How to Lead Work Teams: Facilitation Skills* in 1991, Fran has increasingly focused her work on team development, team leadership, and facilitator training. She consults to a variety of organizations. She designs and facilitates meetings for both public and private organizations and has conducted numerous management development, workforce diversity, mentoring, and train-the-trainer programs.

Fran is the author of four books on the subjects of team leadership and facilitation. She has an M.B.A. from the University of Arizona.

Index